ALSO BY RICHARD SCHOCH

Not Shakespeare

Queen Victoria and the Theatre of Her Age

Shakespeare's Victorian Stage

Victorian Theatrical Burlesques (editor)

THE SECRETS OF HAPPINESS

**Three Thousand Years of
Searching for the Good Life**

RICHARD SCHOCH

SCRIBNER
New York   London   Toronto   Sydney

SCRIBNER
1230 Avenue of the Americas
New York, NY 10020

Originally published in Great Britain in 2006 by Profile Books Ltd

Published by arrangement with Profile Books

First Scribner edition 2006

SCRIBNER and design are trademarks of
Macmillan Library Reference USA, Inc., used under license
by Simon & Schuster, the publisher of this work.

For information about special discounts for bulk purchases,
please contact Simon & Schuster Special Sales:
1-800-456-6798 or business@simonandschuster.com

Designed by Kyoko Watanabe
Set in Minion

Manufactured in the United States of America

1   3   5   7   9   10   8   6   4   2

Library of Congress Cataloging-in-Publication Data

Schoch, Richard W.
The secrets of happiness : three thousand years of searching for the good life /
Richard Schoch.
p.   cm.
Includes bibliographical references and index.
1. Happiness—History. 2. Happiness—Religious aspects—History. I. Title.
BJ1481.S36 2006
170—dc22   2006044375

ISBN-13: 978-0-7432-9292-4
ISBN-10: 0-7432-9292-8

To my mother

CONTENTS

PART IV: ENDURING SUFFERING

THE SECRETS OF
HAPPINESS

INTRODUCTION

Unhappy is the story of happiness. More than two thousand years ago, when the ancient Greeks first thought about what constitutes "the good life," happiness was a civic virtue that demanded a lifetime's cultivation. Now, it's everybody's birthright: swallow a pill, get happy; do yoga, find your bliss; hire a life coach, regain your self-esteem. We have lost contact with the old and rich traditions of happiness, and we have lost the ability to understand their essentially moral nature. Deaf to the conversation of the ages, we deny ourselves the chance of finding a happiness that is meaningful. We've settled, nowadays, for a much weaker, much thinner happiness: mere enjoyment of pleasure, mere avoidance of pain and suffering. The so-called new science of happiness perpetuates this impoverished notion of the good life. Somewhere between Plato and Prozac, happiness stopped being a lofty achievement and became an entitlement.

We can reject this modern enfeeblement of happiness. We can recover its ancient traditions, the traditions that began in the West with the philosophers of Athens and in the East with the anonymous Hindu sages of the Axial Age. We can, with no exaggeration, call these traditions a secret, so unpracticed, if not obscured, have they become. Yet the secret will not resist our attempt to find it.

Over the past decade or so, behavioral scientists, neuroscientists, economists, and psychologists (including a Nobel laureate from Princeton) have been working to measure reported levels of happiness and to identify its causes. Their methods are droll. In one "experience sampling," participants carry Internet-ready palmtop computers twenty-four hours a day. When an alarm sounds on their palmtops, the participants—who have been trained to respond with Pavlovian mechanicity to aural stimulation—stop what they're doing and complete an online survey about how they feel about what they've just stopped doing. Back in the laboratory of happiness, technicians download these data and then plot a graph showing each participant's happiness peaks and troughs over time. In case the guinea pigs have tried to outfox their masters—pretending to be happier or unhappier than they actually are—brain scans are used to confirm their testimony. (The participants, it can be revealed, are honest.)

What do the surveys say? Sex, no surprise, makes everyone feel better. The second best thing is having a drink after work with your friends. Work itself—challenging, rewarding, and secure employment—also contributes greatly to happiness. Commuting, however, makes us miserable. Well, almost all of us; 4 percent of respondents claimed to *enjoy* traffic jams. (Who could these people be?) If you believe the statistics, it's pretty easy to make yourself happy: live within walking distance of an enjoyable and secure job, prop up the bar with your friends, and then go home and have sex. Happiness: the secret revealed!

Happiness is also a growth industry. Self-help books generate $1 billion in annual sales, and the global market for antidepressants (O true apothecary!) stands valued at an astounding $17 billion. The "desire industry"—whose titans are Botox jabbers, personal trainers, and lifestyle gurus—rakes in even more. (So reports the earnestly named Work Foundation.) As a Harvard MBA would say, it's one vast marketing opportunity. At a time when financial prosperity is assured for many, though by no means all, in the industrialized world, happiness has become the ultimate luxury item.

But what *is* this thing called happiness? The scientists and the social scientists do not stop to ask the question because they presume to know its answer. Happiness is . . . well, it's just "feeling good—enjoying life and wanting the feeling to be maintained."[1] So say the economists. In the genial patois of the researchers this is called "subjective well-feeling." Those now in kindergarten, or who once were, will doubtless be familiar with its romping musical expression: "If you're happy and you know it, clap your hands." Maybe the mystery of happiness has *not* been solved by the palmtop experience sampling.

Although the psychologists and the economists offered no satisfactory definition of happiness, they did provide, however unwittingly, a vital clue to its whereabouts. In studies of happiness among Maasai tribes in Kenya, seal hunters in Greenland, and slumdwellers in Calcutta, there was one commonality amid all the diversity: every study began by declaring, sometimes boasting, that it no longer set store by old ways of thinking that have failed to help us find happiness. But once upon a time, when giants walked the earth, these old ways of thinking were known as philosophy and religion.

Over the centuries, benefiting from the law of compound intellectual interest, this deposit of wisdom has grown rich and vast. Some ideas about happiness are philosophical, some are religious; some Eastern, some Western; some thousands of years old, some not a hundred. They take the shape of open letters, secret diaries, self-help manuals, logical treatises, sacred scriptures, and love poems. They are the wise saws to be tested against modern instances. And such is their vitality that without them life seems wasteful and barren. These ideas are the subject of this book.

For most of human history, happiness has been understood, even experienced, in the context of religious belief. Only in the past three or four centuries, and mainly in Western culture, has happiness been divorced, for some people, from faith, religion, and spirituality. So here at the outset we find ourselves at what seems to be an impasse: If so many paths to happiness are bound up in religious belief, doesn't that render them invalid for people of other beliefs, or of none? How can a Christian profit from Hindu teachings on happiness? Why should an atheist bother to read the works of an Islamic mystic?

In writing this book, I have assumed that the purpose of encountering other religious traditions is not conversion, but enlightenment. And that is the spirit in which I invite you to read it. By enlightenment, I mean an appreciative recognition that another's beliefs, traditions, or culture can reveal, can offer up, an insight that will enhance one's own beliefs, traditions, or culture. Even if we cannot fully enter into someone else's beliefs, still we can learn from them. I suspect that this answer may be unsatisfying to some readers (no doubt because it appears to smack of a politically correct piety), but I believe that if we approach the pursuit of happiness too parochially, we will succeed only in denying ourselves something of value.

Like all great ideas, those about happiness, no matter their origin, flow from minds attuned to universals, minds quickened by concerns so basic to our being that we ignore them to our cost. What human creature, even at the risk of a despairing insight, has never inquired into the nature—and possibility—of his or her own happiness? To introduce some of those great ideas, I want to tell you the story of three people who, long ago and far away, in moments of trauma and terrible strain, reflected profoundly about happiness—and then allowed those reflections to suffuse their lives with purpose and meaning. Later, I expand on the stories, giving to each its own proper chapter, and I tell other stories in other chapters, too. For the purposes of this introduction, though, I want to use them as our preliminary examples, our first glimpses of what it means to search for happiness. We may not share the lonely burdens of these extraordinary characters, or their ferocious courage, but we are dashed by the same troubles and can be restored by the same consolations.

Epicurus

Epicurus (341–271 B.C.), if you believe his critics, of whom there have been many throughout history, was a fellow of a most scandalous course of life. Yet even his most aggressive detractors would concede that he was exceptionally clever. A philosopher in ancient Athens, he preached in the city's open marketplace, the *agora,* that the sole source of happiness is pleasure. (The ancient Greek word for pleasure was *hedone,* from which we derive the modern word "hedonist.") Pleasure, because it is the key to happiness, must be the ultimate aim of our every action: whatever we do, we should do it for pleasure. Epicurus believed that we should embrace pleasure because Nature herself had planted within all of us the desire for it. In a fundamentally healthy way, pleasure is good.

Still, Epicurus preferred to take his pleasures in private. Retreating from society, he founded a quasi-religious cult that survived him by seven centuries and flourished in every part of the Mediterranean world from Herod's Judaea to Caesar's Gaul. It began slowly. Epicurus and his disciples, who wore signet rings bearing his image and committed to memory his precepts and injunctions, retreated to a secret garden outside Athens. There, in splendid isolation, they heeded the call to "live the obscure life": to renounce luxury, to abstain from sensual indulgence, and, most uncharacteristically for inhabitants of democracy's birthplace, to disclaim their civic duties.

But it was the tragic fate of Epicurus to be misunderstood. Partly because his enclave dared to include women—who were politically and intellectually disenfranchised—and partly because it was cut off from the Athenian city-state, outsiders formed a sharply negative picture of this philosophical separatist movement and its mesmerizing leader. Epicurus was accused, among other transgressions, of holding orgies with "Baby Lion," "Little Conquest," and "Tits," among the most glamorous courtesans of their day. Three centuries after his death, this "foul-mouthed bastard," as the Roman philosopher Epictetus branded him, was still being condemned for moral depravity.

The fact of the matter is that Epicureanism, properly understood, promotes none of the self-indulgence and extravagance that have been so detrimentally attributed to it over the centuries. Epicurus, if we look closely, was a generous, reverent, and patriotic Athenian. We need only read the man's letters and proverbs (some of which are, bizarrely, preserved in the Vatican) to discover that Epicurus taught that the good life requires discipline and restraint.

Once, in all sincerity, he asked his friend Idomeneus to send him a slice of cheese "so that when I want to have a feast I shall be able to do so."[2] He claimed that no one's life was ever improved by having an orgasm. He spoke without guile (although his claim must cast into doubt the pride of Baby Lion). Yes, Epicurus believed that pleasure was the secret of happiness, but here's the twist: he defined pleasure not as sensual indulgence—touching this, tasting that—but as the absence of desire. That's where his innumerable critics (Cicero, honorably apart) got him wrong. True pleasure, Epicurus insisted, is marked not by intensity but by tranquility. Happiness, profound and lasting, is the calm after the storm.

Seneca

In Córdoba, Spain, a few years before the birth of Jesus Christ, was born the greatest expositor of Roman Stoicism. His name was Lucius Annaeus Seneca (4 B.C.–A.D. 65). The talented son of a prominent father, he was educated in Rome, where he remained to pursue a career in government. Despite his advantages, and his eventual prominence, Seneca did not have an easy life.

The Emperor Claudius banished him to the island of Corsica (an inhospitable and uncivilized place, where Latin was only rarely heard), mistakenly believing that Seneca had committed adultery with the emperor's own niece. Eventually, Seneca was restored to his position at the imperial court, where he exercised vast powers and amassed great riches under the rule of the next emperor, the infamous Nero. But it was not long before Nero turned his honorable counselor into a dirty thug. Seneca was forced to plot the assassination of Nero's mother—at Nero's unloving behest—and then to justify the crime before the Roman Senate. Finally, Seneca was ordered to kill himself when the paranoid emperor suspected him of treachery. Though innocent, Seneca had no choice but to do a tyrant's bidding.

In the years of banishment, in the times of upheaval, and, finally, in the days before his death, Seneca could not help but wonder why bad things happen to blameless people. If the universe is unjust, how can anyone be sure of finding happiness? The question is grievously perennial. Job, the suffering servant of the Hebrew God, asked much the same. The anguished Seneca, going one step further, answered this seemingly unanswerable question.

Through bombastic and emotionally overwrought adaptations of Greek tragedies he rendered in dramatic form the abrupt reversals of fortune that visited him over the years. But Seneca's most extended reflections, which arose, undeniably, from the pain and misery of his life, are found in his more dignified philosophical writings: dialogues, treatises, and personal addresses of consolation and advice to friends and relatives. Faced with impossible moral dilemmas, Seneca took refuge in the Stoic values of detachment and indifference and found that those values could bring him happiness even in circumstances more dreadful than he could have imagined. Addressing himself as much as his readers, Seneca explained that happiness "can only be achieved by having first, a sound mind in constant possession of its soundness; then a brave and energetic mind, which is also gifted with the noblest form of endurance; able to deal with circumstances of the moment. . . . Everlasting freedom and tranquility follow once we have banished all that vexes and frightens us."[3]

In a spirit of detachment, Seneca calmly awaited a fate whose horrible course he was powerless to alter. Throughout life, his goal had been to harness the mind's rational powers so that he might withstand both the injuries that had been so unfairly and so relentlessly inflicted on him *and* the seductive charms of good fortune. So often, and perhaps more than we would like to admit, we trick ourselves into believing that happiness depends on good fortune. That is a tempting, but ultimately damaging, way to think because it absolves you and me from the responsibility to create happiness in whatever circumstances we face.

Seneca did not think that way. Emboldened by the Stoic belief that happiness is independent of mere circumstance, he accepted the "blessings of fortune" without embarrassment or shame, yet remained fully prepared to relinquish them at a moment's notice.[4] When that inevitable moment came—first in exile to Corsica, and later in anxious retirement—he gave up without a struggle every last thing that he possessed, including his own life. But one thing has survived: the pattern of Seneca's noble life, and that belongs to posterity.

Ghazali

In Baghdad, toward the end of the eleventh century, an acclaimed Islamic scholar fell mysteriously ill, renounced his career, and spent two years praying alone in a mosque in Damascus. His name was Abu Hamid al-Ghazali (1058–1111). Born in the Persian city of Tûs, Ghazali grew up to be an authority on religious law, in recognition of which he was honored with the titles "The Proof of Islam" and "The Ornament of Faith." At the young age of thirty-three he was appointed to a professorship at the Nizamiyya college in Baghdad. Shortly after reaching this position of intellectual eminence he fell victim to a debilitating spiritual crisis. It turned out to be the first step in his quest for happiness, a quest that would take him to distant lands over many years.

At the height of his worldly success Ghazali realized, to his shame, that he was too much with the world, too entangled in its strangulating net. He doubted the worth of the subjects he taught and admitted, if only to himself, that his motivation for teaching was the basest of all motives: pride. Firm in his faith, Ghazali knew, nonetheless, that he would be denied eternal life in paradise if he could not discipline his desires and relinquish his attachment to worldly goods. As he lived in fear and indecision, the crisis worsened. One day, standing before his students, about to give a lecture, he suddenly lost the power of speech. Soon he could not swallow food. His doctor diagnosed an "ailment of the heart." Ghazali, who possessed the soul of a poet, interpreted the clinical findings allegorically: his physical illness was the emblem of his underlying spiritual illness. He stood in danger not of losing his mortal body (that would perish eventually anyway) but of losing something far more precious: his immortal soul.

Just as the crisis was extreme, so was its cure. At the pinnacle of his fame Ghazali abandoned his career, his friends, and his wealth. After setting aside money for his sons' education and entrusting them to the care of relatives (how it must have pained him to say good-bye), he traveled to Damascus, where he spent the next two years in reflection and religious devotion. Geography, alas, prevented the happy coincidence of Ghazali journeying along the same road where, a millennium earlier, St. Paul underwent his own conversion. The minaret in the Umayyad mosque where he prayed in solitude became known as "the Ghazali minaret." Through the habit of meditation he became convinced, not in his mind but in his innermost being, that only through direct personal experience could he find the joy that comes from knowing God. Ghazali recovered from his spiritual crisis not through his own strength but through a transcendent one: the light of God shining into his heart.

Ghazali's crisis coincided with his introduction to Sufism, the mystical side of Islam that preaches neither doctrine nor dogma but affirms, above all else, the transforming power of the personal experience of God's presence. The Sufis call this experience *dhawq,* "taste," which nicely captures the sensuous immediacy of their vision of happiness. (As the Sufis say, "He who tastes, knows.") Surprisingly, this reverence for firsthand experience appealed to a man whose entire life had been devoted to impersonal theories and abstractions. Renouncing, as it were, his confidence in speculative reason, Ghazali vowed to "walk in the mystic way" so that he might encounter the transcendent wisdom whose only source was lived experience. Although we may never travel down that same path, we have probably all felt the need to know something from inside ourselves: to feel it, as the saying goes, in our bones. Our own hunger for knowledge deeper than logic, more intimate than reason and rationality, can help us to understand why Ghazali felt compelled to walk in the mystic way.

What he learned from his conversion to mysticism Ghazali recorded in *The Alchemy of Happiness,* a short book of moral guidance written in Persian for a popular audience. The clue to the secret of happiness lies in the title. Just as the alchemist transforms base metals into precious ones—lead into gold—we can transform our vices into virtues. In the alchemy of happiness we become the best possible version of ourselves, the most precious form of our rough (but ready) matter.

The lives of Epicurus, Seneca, and Ghazali seem to defy nearly every attempt at pattern detection. Certainly no pattern is detectable in location: a walled garden outside ancient Athens, the court of the Emperor

Nero, and a mosque in Damascus. Spanning fourteen hundred years, these stories encompass classical Greek culture, Rome in its imperial decadence, and an Islamic civilization that stretched from India to Spain. Ghazali alone invokes a specific religious tradition. Epicurus was content to leave the Greek gods on top of Mount Olympus because they were content to ignore what happened below. No doubt Seneca worshipped the Roman equivalent of the Greek deities, but he did not call on them in his moment of need. On the face of things, little connects a Greek philosopher with a cult following of prostitutes, a Roman civil servant forced to commit suicide, and a Persian scholar who traded books for mystic ecstasy.

But the face of things is not the basis of things. When we look at the world's great thinkers about happiness we are bound to find them different in time, different in place, different in language and culture. Inevitable though these differences are, they cannot obscure the deep similarities in how we search for happiness. The stories of Epicurus, Seneca, and Ghazali resonate with us today, thousands of years later, because they are, in truth, our own stories. Within them, we find not enigmatic figures from an alien past, but magnified—*magnificent*—versions of ourselves. From even these initial examples, these first few accounts of courageous seekers, we can learn some lasting truths about the pursuit of happiness. (In the Epicurean manner, I'll phrase them as proverbs.) And that in itself will take us a long way toward clarifying just what the search for happiness means. If we're not clear about that, the searching—and the finding—cannot even begin.

Catch Big Fish

On a large wooden plaque that hung for many years in my father's study was mounted a blue-tailed dolphin that he had caught when deep-sea fishing off the Florida coast. It turned out to be the biggest fish he ever caught, and so it was the only one he ever displayed. Its trophy status was never in jeopardy. The search for happiness is something like that. It's about reeling in the "big fish"—the only kind that truly matters—even if it means a lot of struggle.

Epicurus, Seneca, and Ghazali all fished in deep waters. They shared a commitment to discovering the ultimate ends and purposes of life (the ancients called this *telos*), and they believed in the importance of leading a life that was worthwhile. In different ways, they all reflected on the shape, the *character,* of their lives as a whole. Out of that reflection dawned the insight that their lives, if they were to be better, would have to change. Epicurus knew that to achieve the tranquility that would lead to happiness he would have to withdraw from society and seek solace in his pastoral retreat, even though it meant that his reputation would be sullied by false allegations of moral depravity. Instead of raging against injustice or descending into self-pity, Seneca turned adversity into triumph by accepting his fate with a calm and tranquil mind. Ghazali, afflicted with an inner torment, recognized that his declining health was a divine summons to cure his sickened soul by embracing a new way of life.

These moments of reckoning all occurred under harrowing conditions: calumny, injustice, and emotional collapse. Mercifully, you and I will probably be spared such torments. That doesn't mean, however, that we don't have our own moments of reckoning; we just have them in ways commensurate with the rest of our lives. It would be extraordinary for any of us suddenly to quit our job, leave our family, and move to a new country, yet we can still appreciate why a man in Baghdad nearly a thousand years ago felt compelled to do just that. We can catch in him a glimpse of ourselves. In Ghazali's dilemma we recognize a serious version of that psychotherapeutic cliché, the midlife crisis: the frightening, perhaps even debilitating prospect that the life we have so carefully built over the years is without purpose and without value. Far from being a historical curiosity of only passing interest, Ghazali's heroic effort to restore meaning to his life is a distant mirror of our own attempts to straighten out the mess in our lives.

Not too long ago there was a newspaper report about a man who became a millionaire in the lottery yet spent all his winnings in the first year or so and then got himself arrested on a drug charge. Clearly this man was no happier despite the short-term pleasure he derived from his financial windfall. The sense of waste that characterizes this story (all that money, and he did *what*?) naturally invites comparison, usually of a self-flattering kind. You might wonder whether such extreme good fortune would make *you* happy. What you probably have in mind is not the pleasure and enjoyment of winning lots of money (you take that for granted) but the way the money could transform your life. You wonder whether you would have made *better* use of the money. To think like that is to think about the quality of your life as a whole: you understand your life as a series of actions and you know that some actions are better than others.

Thinking about life as a whole is intimately tied to making decisions and taking action. When we arrive at the inevitable crossroads of life, we must choose a direction. Do I marry—or forsake—this person? Do I honor—or betray—my friends? Do I tell—or conceal—the truth? We should not decide such things blindly (yet how often we do just that); we should decide them in light of how we understand our life in its entirety. We should think about what we want our life to be like, and then we should act accordingly. Everyone's search for happiness demands this kind of big fish thinking. And yet how hard it is for us to be self-aware even for a moment, let alone a lifetime.

Little fish—nice feelings, good moods, raw pleasures—do still matter, only not as much as we might ordinarily suppose. We all know what obviously happy moments are like; they're the times when everything's great and all that we desire lies within our grasp. Fortunately, there's no end to the experiences that make us feel good: gazing into the eyes of our beloved, scoring the winning goal in a soccer game, swimming in the ocean (Camus thought this was one of the most intense forms of happiness he had ever known), or being swept up and carried away by a rapturous piece of music. These are the kinds of incidents that joyfully crowd our lives and make them wonderful. More, please.

But do they make us happy? And if so, how much happiness do they provide? The late philosopher Robert Nozick described pleasurable experiences as "how life feels from the inside."[5] He meant, of course, the warmth, the glow, that radiates inside us when we enjoy life. Just think of that eloquent gesture of contemporary self-expression, the airpunch. It's the spontaneous outward sign of irrepressible inward delight. Winning athletes do it when they learn they've won. Talk show audiences do it when a guest jubilantly confesses, without a whisper of self-reproach, to some barely legal perversion. We've all done it.

Yet no matter how wonderful "life feels from the inside," such feelings are only the *beginning* of happiness, not its ultimate destination. As Nozick elaborated, we care about many things other than pleasurable experiences. We care about the integrity of our values and beliefs. We care about our accomplishments. We care about leaving a legacy to the world. We care about the well-being of the people in our lives. And, if we're truly magnanimous, we care about the well-being of people *not* in our lives. All these cares bind us to the world—through what we believe, what we achieve, and whom we love. This is the ultimately *moral* shape of each person's happiness and what makes it inseparable from—in truth, dependent on—the happiness of others. Happiness may, and probably will, begin with pleasurable feelings, but it will also go well beyond them because happiness isn't really about feeling good—it's about being good. The problem is that we are apt to mistake the former for the latter.

It was, ironically, the twentieth century's most influential econo-mist, John Maynard Keynes, who insisted that material prosperity could never confer on individuals the *purposiveness,* as he called it, that is a necessary part of happiness. In 1928, in a lecture on "Economic Possibilities for Our Grandchildren," Keynes predicted that when humanity was at last freed from the bondage of poverty and depriva-tion (a freedom that appeared near on the horizon to the generation between the world wars) it would face the existential challenge of using its material freedom "to live wisely and agreeably and well." Who would rise up to meet this challenge? Not the getters and the spenders, but those who "cultivate into a fuller perfection, the art of life itself." Keynes then made a daring leap into the morality of happiness: the "art of life," he explained, consists in being "more concerned with the remote future results of our actions than with their own quality or their imme-diate effects on our own environment."[6] Happiness, that is, means more than pleasing ourselves. It means pleasing others, especially the others we are destined never to know.

Wrestle, Don't Dance

Marcus Aurelius ruled the Roman Empire from A.D. 161 to 180, and spent many of those years fighting off foreign invasion in northern Italy and Germany. It was during these harsh military campaigns that Marcus recorded his thoughts in a private document that he titled *To Myself*. Written in Greek, the language of the examined life, the emperor's moral diary is better known to posterity as the *Meditations*. Part of what has ensured that over eighteen centuries this book has never lacked for readers is that its author knew how to turn a phrase. When talking about abstract things, Marcus used lively and unusual images. His favorite one for happiness was wrestling.

A life-long warrior, Marcus certainly spent many hours wrestling, as it was one of the dominant aspects of Greco-Roman masculine culture. So, like any good writer, Marcus drew on his experience. More important though, the choice reveals how he understood happiness. In one of his most insightful passages he explains that happiness feels more like wrestling than dancing because it requires us to "stand prepared and unshaken to meet what comes and what we did not foresee."[7] Later in the work, he commanded himself to wrestle to become the kind of man he wished himself to be.

Marcus's words are tough and unforgiving, and they were meant to be. If that old soldier had written with more refinement, more delicacy, we wouldn't believe him and he wouldn't have believed himself. It takes a hardness of language to make the hard point that you have to keep working at happiness. You don't just arrive at a blissful destination and then stay there for the rest of your days. Happiness doesn't just happen; it must be prepared for, cultivated, sustained. Over and over again, the match must be refought and the victory gained anew.

Perhaps, as his thoughts turned to wrestling, Marcus had been dreaming of Aristotle. For it was the Greek rationalist who insisted, in his *Nicomachean Ethics,* that we are created for happiness, that it is the ultimate goal of your life, my life, and everyone else's. But it was also Aristotle who owned up to the disconcerting fact that happiness does not come to us easily. Just as "one swallow does not make a summer," he reasoned, one pleasant day does not make a whole life happy. And so in the next breath Aristotle called happiness an *activity*. By that he meant that it requires skill, concentration, and focus. Far from being a state of passive enjoyment, like relaxing in a bubble bath or eating a box of chocolates, happiness demands active effort.

Being happy, then, is something that we resolve to achieve rather than something pleasant that comes our way like sunshine after a rainstorm. (The psychologist Mihalyi Csikszentmihalyi has similarly argued that the basis of happiness is "flow," a state of concentration and heightened attentiveness that we make happen in life.) To strive for happiness means not simply that you would like to be happy—who doesn't?—but that you regard your life as a journey on which you move purposefully toward that ultimate goal. Or, to use Marcus's image, becoming happy is like winning a wrestling match.

Epicurus, Seneca, and Ghazali all knew something about wrestling for happiness, about winning a better life for themselves in circumstances not in their favor. But even in lives more ordinary—*our* lives, here and now—we must still wrestle for our happiness. We need only think of moments such as taking a marriage vow (or, indeed, any kind of vow), when we pledge our future and then struggle to honor that pledge. To marry someone is to sign up for a new kind of life in the full—and unsettling—knowledge that this entails renouncing both a former life and all other possible lives. In choosing each other, the bride and groom forsake everyone else (for that is what it means to choose), not just for today but for all the tomorrows that they have left together. When couples renew their marriage vows it is not, obviously, because their vows have expired in the way that a library card expires. It is because they wish to rededicate themselves to a union that they cherish even more strongly. The struggle is not a barrier to happiness (Thank goodness the struggle is over. Now we can dance!). This is the kind of joyful struggle that *is* happiness.

Start at the Beginning

Everyone's journey to happiness begins from the same place: unhappiness. We start, all of us, with the feeling that our lives are out of joint, no matter how stable and fastened they appear. We might be unsure how to repair it, but we sense the misalignment between the life we have and the life we imagine ourselves to have. This is the lovers' quarrel we have with life.

Rarely is our first step toward happiness a giant one. Sometimes we may not even recognize that we are taking it. A few years ago, the journalist David Brooks wrote an amusing book called *Bobos in Paradise*. Bobos are "Bourgeois Bohemians," the new elite that emerged out of the dot.com revolution of the 1990s. Brooks argued that, unlike previous generations of successful entrepreneurs, Bobos seek to unite the economic values of capitalism with the social values of the 1960s counterculture. The more Brooks studied Bobos, the more he saw the paradox governing their lives: they feel dissatisfied, despite their professional success and material comfort. These evangelists for the gospel of unlimited choice found that they were still searching for something.

On a Sunday afternoon a few months ago I went to a Shaker furniture store. The place was filled with affluent Bobos buying expensive chairs, dressers, and tables meant to look simple, homespun, and rustic. The customers were trying to connect themselves to the values that the furniture symbolizes. They weren't buying only a four-poster bed, they were also buying the *idea* behind the four-poster bed. (Plato would approve.) The purchase was part of the search for what had gone missing in their lives. Of course, you could say this is true of all conspicuous consumption: that we buy things to fill a gap in our lives, to make us feel more genuine, more authentic, more real.

Bobos are hardly the first people to search for something missing in their lives. The question they face—How do I invest my life with meaning?—is a perennial one. Indeed, it is *the* human question. And behind it lies a general truth about the search for happiness. The truth is that being dissatisfied is a necessary step, the *first* step, toward being happy.

When I set out to explore happiness I didn't know what I would find. That's what it means to explore. But I was pretty sure what I *wouldn't* find. Although it's been possible to grasp a few general principles about how to orient our shared search for happiness, I had no expectation of discovering a grand theory that applies to everyone in all times and across all cultures. I did not look to find it because I did not think it was there to be found. It would be naïve to expect that the Hebrew Bible, Greek philosophy, the Koran, the Hindu Upanishads, and Buddha's Four Noble Truths, to cite just a few works of ancient wisdom about happiness, could be compressed into one single idea about the good life.

"Happy families are all alike," Tolstoy wrote in the famous first line of *Anna Karenina*. He got it pretty much wrong. The statement "I am happy" (or "I am unhappy") carries no *objective* meaning—that is, independent of the person, the subject, making the statement— because it acquires meaning only in a context. Indeed, it must mean something different to every person who utters it. Which explains why all attempts to *measure* happiness are ludicrous, as if it were some mass-produced commodity that we could stockpile in times of lazy contentment and then raid in moments of urgent need. (The scientists would, perhaps, insist that *I* am wrong and Tolstoy right.)

Happiness is less an objective fact to be encountered in the world than an experience to be cultivated by each one of us. Thus, we may speak not of any single secret of happiness, applicable to everyone, but only of the *secrets* of happiness—a different one for each person. This is true in an obvious way for people separated by time and place. The happiness of an ancient Greek cannot be entirely the same as that of a modern Greek (or a modern anybody), just as the happiness of a Muslim cannot be shared by an atheist. And yet each can be happy in his or her way.

Moreover, happiness is never identical even for people united by culture and community. Because individuals face trials and tests that are uniquely theirs, their happiness rises up in a correspondingly unique way. Your happiness belongs to you and to you alone. If we think of happiness as something that we make in life, and not as something that we find elsewhere and then import into life, we can see, without much difficulty, that any proclamation of happiness must refer back to the individual who proclaims it. So we ought to be less concerned about ironclad definitions, about fitting happiness into precise categories, and more focused on simply making it happen. For although it cannot be deduced theoretically, happiness can be conjured in the moment of our experience.

The odd thing about happiness, then, is that this global phenomenon never acts on the world stage, but only ever makes local appearances. So although there is no unchanging idea of happiness, the term itself encompasses a range of meanings, some of which are bound to be inconsistent. A concept of happiness that appears natural to one culture or historical moment may appear alien to another. Indeed, some versions of happiness are simply irreconcilable: Stoics train themselves to rely on reason, and religious mystics free themselves from reason's shackle; utilitarians insist on maximizing pleasure, and Buddhists strive to detach themselves from desire. Not all approaches to happiness are equally practical: Hinduism places a strong emphasis on the duties and responsibilities of everyday life, and Christianity emphasizes that we cannot become truly happy on our own because we need the gift of God's grace. In the chapters to come, we shall see all these differences and more. But the differences arise not because the paths to happiness are insufficient or incomplete (those demerits belong, unfortunately, to *us*) but because being different is part of what it means to belong to your own culture and to exist in your own time.

Still, there is unity in diversity. The differences do not fall beyond the circumference of our understanding. Every conception of the good life that has emerged throughout history, in whatever culture, takes up the same four themes: pleasure, desire, reason, and suffering. These are the irreducible elements of our happiness, its fundamental shape, its indelible texture. These are the things we reckon with as we strive to become happy. But we reckon with them in a particular way: we must be able to moderate pleasure, to control desire, to transcend (or rely on) reason, and to endure suffering. The examples in this introduction begin to show us how the reckoning takes place. Epicurus picked his pleasures carefully, and so controlled his desires; Seneca used reason's strength to protect him from adversity; Ghazali found the hidden meaning that lies beyond reason. In the chapters ahead we will look at still further examples of how to create happiness in the circumstances of life as we live it here and now.

Be they ancient or modern, Eastern or Western, religious or secular, all visions of happiness focus on these few enduring existential dilemmas and differ only in the manner, marvelously kaleidoscopic, of mixing and applying them. These multiple visions do not betray any weakness in happiness but consecrate its power, like that of some fantastical, yet benevolent, shape-shifter, to suit the exigencies of the time.

If we listen patiently to the wisdom of the ages, we will hear, faintly at first, and then ever more loudly, a single and sustained refrain, played in different keys and tuned to different pitches, but still, and always, the same resounding chords. Should we be disappointed that, unlike the universe, happiness does *not* expand infinitely? Let us instead rejoice that happiness may well be the one thing that can resist unpredictability. For however happiness arises in our life, it must do so in the context of perennial, not accidental, let alone unexpected, concerns; whatever it is about, it is about a few constant things: pleasure, desire, reason, and suffering. The secrets to happiness lie here, and nowhere else.

You probably will not read this book to absorb vast amounts of history, philosophy, and theology (although it is there for the absorption-minded). You will read it, more likely, to be inspired by the greatest ideas in history about happiness and to discover how they might transform your life. Such a yearning led me to write this book. So my hope is that you will use it to reflect on the project of your life; to ask yourself, unblinkingly, whether you are leading the good life; to become, in short, the philosopher of your own happiness.

PART I

Living for Pleasure

1

THE GREATEST HAPPINESS
(THE UTILITARIANS)

The eighteenth-century English legal philosopher Jeremy Bentham (1748–1832) unveiled his hyperrational theory of happiness in a monumental work of jurisprudence for which he wrote the introduction but nothing else. We cannot charge the man with laziness, as the introduction ran to more than three hundred pages. Still, Bentham was reluctant to publish it, knowing that he was capable of even more. His less cautious friend, George Wilson, a Scottish barrister, urged him to have the essay printed without delay, because a rival scholar's impending publication threatened to make Bentham's own work redundant. Moreover, drafts of his other essays were already in circulation, and it would not be long before some enterprising but unscrupulous scholar stole his ideas. At last Bentham agreed, warily, that his "dry and tedious" work should be set before the public.[1] By this time, however, the rats that infested Bentham's modest law chambers had begun to devour the original manuscript. The author quickly rescued his work, bundled it off to the printer, and promptly published the uneaten portions as *An Introduction to the Principles of Morals and Legislation* (1791).

The title is misleading, for the book is not a study of morals and leg-islation; it is, rather, an almanac of crime and punishment. (Bentham, who spent a lot of time thinking about criminals, designed a prison where all inmates could be placed under constant surveillance. Com-missioned, but rejected, by Parliament, it was called the Panopticon, Greek for "all-seeing.") Oddly, Bentham's book on crime and punish-ment is his lasting contribution to the pursuit of happiness, for in its pages he explains how we can attain happiness through rationally cho-sen pleasures. Bentham's dreary name for the pleasure principle was *utility,* a word that in his day connoted not usefulness, but satisfaction: when an object "produce[s] benefit, advantage, pleasure, good, or hap-piness," words that for Bentham were all synonyms.[2] Rationality is the key to understanding why utilitarian theory remains today so power-fully attractive: it explains happiness logically, clearly, and completely. For every question you want to ask, Bentham's model provides an answer.

Bentham's primary concern was the social environment in which we all strive to maximize our utility (or pleasure) and thus increase our happiness. *How* anyone should pursue happiness was best left to the individual concerned. Still, somebody has to ensure that the pursuit is possible in the first place, and that is the government's job: to create the conditions that allow all of us to seek happiness in whatever way we think best. So Bentham wrote his *Introduction* with politicians in mind (hence the numbing bureaucratic tone), and he was keen to give them everything they needed to know about happiness so that they could pass laws to promote it. That, beyond question, remains the profound and lasting influence of utilitarianism on how we think of happiness: that it is not undertaken in isolation but always through contact with other people, always in the civic arena. And that means that everyone's pursuit of happiness can be helped or hindered by that meddlesome creature called government.

The Greatest Happiness

In the year that Thomas Jefferson wrote "the pursuit of happiness" into the founding document of American liberty, Bentham, on the other side of the Atlantic, committed himself to the principle of "the greatest happiness of the greatest number." What Bentham meant, first of all, was that the rightness (or wrongness) of an action depends entirely on its *consequences,* not on the action itself nor the motives of the actor. The rule of thumb is this: in any circumstance, the morally right action is the one that produces the best outcome. The best outcome is the one that "augment[s] the happiness of the community."[3] For Bentham, the more happiness an action produces, the more preferable it becomes.

Though he took an inclusive approach to happiness, Bentham still defined it in traditionally hedonistic terms: maximizing pleasure and minimizing pain. Indeed, he begins the *Introduction* by asserting that pleasure and pain "govern us in all we do, in all we say, in all we think."[4] It's hard to imagine a statement more sweeping about our lives than that. Because pleasure controls "all we do," it cannot be merely passive contentment or submissive enjoyment; rather, it must involve action, deliberate and overt. Pleasure, then, is volitional: what we *will* to do. (This meaning is not entirely foreign to us, because the word "pleasure" still carries a residual sense of intention. In Britain, prisoners are detained "at Her Majesty's pleasure" not because the queen enjoys throwing people into jail but because she *wills* their imprisonment, as the proper punishment for their crimes.) Also, pleasure is absolute. There is no greater goal than pleasure, nor anything other than pleasure we would strive to obtain. It's not as if you prefer to maximize pleasure while I prefer justice. No, we *both* want pleasure and we want it all the time.

The Catalog of Pleasure

Anyone who believes that happiness consists in securing more pleasure than pain ought to have an encyclopedic knowledge on the matter. To such knowledge Bentham aspired, and his zeal for tabulating, organizing, and classifying data is nowhere more apparent than in the *Introduction,* where he offers an impressively detailed account of pleasures and pains, their sources, their variations, and our motives for attaining or avoiding them. In a phrase that now strikes an unintended note of lechery, he called it his "catalog of pleasure."

Apart from its slightly archaic language, Bentham's roster reads just as we would expect: wealth, power, and skill rank high among the pleasures, and their opposites—privation, enmity, and awkwardness—are the chief pains. Merely to glance at Bentham's hedonic inventory is to recognize that he permitted only quantitative distinctions (*more* and *less*) between pleasures. Qualitative distinctions (*better* and *worse*) had no standing. Thus, as long as the resulting quantity of pleasure was the same, the child's game of pushpin, he declared, was just as good as poetry. A blunt egalitarianism is at work here: equal amounts of pleasure are equally worthwhile, no matter their source. Whether it be throwing darts, composing sonnets, or torturing kittens (some people *do* like that sort of thing), no one kind of pleasure is intrinsically superior to another. That kind of blanket statement is likely to worry us because it allows all sorts of bad behavior to march under the banner of pleasure. Eventually, it worried Bentham, too.

Crunching the Numbers

To know whether we are as happy as we can be, Bentham devised his "felicific calculus," or happiness equation. Put simply, *happiness equals pleasure minus pain.* Of course, it is misleading to state matters so simply, especially when it took Bentham hundreds of pages to explain the equation's hidden intricacies. The first step in calculating happiness is to weigh all the pleasures and pains in our life. This is more complicated than just putting them on a scale (what would that scale look like?) because we need to know various things about them: their aspects, the circumstances affecting them, and how they relate to each other. To begin with the aspects, or essential characteristics: intensity, duration, certainty, propinquity, fecundity, purity, and extent—these are the factors that determine *how much* pleasure or pain arises from a given action.

The aspects are more commonsensical than they seem. Intensity and duration are the basic properties of all pleasures and pains: a certain force (intensity) exerted over a certain time (duration). We must also, however, account for pleasures and pains that have yet to occur because we do have anticipatory feelings about them, whether looking forward to a vacation or fearing the dentist's drill. In considering future pleasures and pains, we assign a value to both their likelihood (certainty) and their time frame (propinquity). The more certain you are to be promoted, for example, the more pleasure you will derive from thinking about it, and as the date of your advancement draws nearer, the more excited you become.

We must also have regard for fecundity and purity, the side effects of pleasure and pain. Fecundity, or fruitfulness, refers to the likelihood that a sensation will duplicate itself: that pleasure will beget more pleasure, or pain more pain. Purity, however, refers to the likelihood that a sensation will *not* be followed by its opposite, but will remain its own "pure" self: pleasure will not lead to pain, nor pain give rise to pleasure. Finally, we must determine how much our pleasures and pains affect others. To employ Bentham's term, we want to know their *extent*. When parents take pride in their children's achievements, or suffer sympathetically when they fall ill, the initial pleasure or pain extends outward to them, like ripples spreading across a lake.

Bentham penned a few lines to remind readers of these aspects of pleasure and pain:

> *Intense, long, certain, speedy, fruitful, pure—*
> *Such marks in pleasures and in pains endure.*
> *Such pleasures seek, if private be thy end:*
> *If it be public, wide let them extend.*
> *Such pains avoid, whichever be thy view:*
> *If pains must come, let them extend to few.*[5]

Enough abstraction: let us put this theory to work. Suppose you want to know how much happiness you derive from gardening. First, you assign a value to each relevant pleasure: the satisfaction of achievement, the tranquility of the work, the warmth of the sun, and, of course, the beauty of the flowers themselves. Then you add them up to determine the sum total of your pleasure. Next, you follow the same procedure, but with respect to each pain: blistered hands, stiff knees, bee stings, the bothersome sight of weeds, and the toxic fumes of insect repellent. Finally, you subtract the total value of pain from the total value of pleasure. The sum left over is your happiness (or unhappiness). If the final number is greater than zero, then you are happy, and the higher the number, the happier you are. Keep on planting. But if your balance is negative, then you are unhappy, and the greater the deficit, the more profound your misery. Put down the trowel now.

For simplicity's sake, I have left out something important: the *effect* that your garden has on other people. Because, like all of us, you seek the greatest happiness of the greatest number, you can't get away with saying that *you* derive pleasure from gardening and nobody else matters. Other people *do* matter, and in their collectivity they matter more than you do. So the real question becomes: Does your garden make the *community* happy? To figure that out you must go back and repeat all the pleasure and pain calculations for all the people who have looked over the fence into your garden. True, these calculations will become increasingly complex if people have different reactions (they love it, they hate it), you are unable to determine their reactions (they don't tell you), or you don't know how many people to factor into the equation (so many have looked in that you've lost track). Yet only by performing these calculations can you know with certainty how much happiness your actions create for the entire community.

It is reassuring to pursue happiness in a rational and ordered way; the logic of it makes us believe that the pursuit will be successful, if only we turn our minds to it. Bentham understood, however, that we could not, each of us, spend so much time calculating the odds for happiness that we never get around to doing the things that actually make us happy. In fact, he never imagined that the general public would use the felicific calculus. Rather, he intended it to be a tool for politicians, to help them pass laws to maximize general levels of happiness. As Bentham explained, the calculus's true purpose is to apportion happiness throughout the community (rather like Santa Claus distributing toys). If we leave to the politicians all these intricate rules, complex formulae, and unwieldy calculations, we can simply get on with being happy.

Legislating Happiness

From the political theorists of the English Civil War—Thomas Hobbes, author of *Leviathan* (1651), most notably—Bentham inherited the belief that governments exist to form stable and peaceful civil societies as the best alternative to the state of nature. But those who govern need to be taught how, and Bentham appointed himself their tutor. Not even the most tireless lawmaker, however, could possibly determine *all* the actions required to maximize the happiness of *all* the people. Happiness must be achieved at something faster than a snail's pace. Bentham's advice to politicians was that if they got the big things right, then all the little things would fall into place. Getting the big things right means protecting each citizen's life and property: you cannot be happy if your life is endangered or your property at risk. Indeed, you would gladly spend the time and incur the expense necessary to prevent risk or harm to either. *That* is the responsibility of government and the reason you sacrificed some of your natural liberty to create it in the first place. So we now have a definition of good government: one that allows you to sleep easily at night, trusting that your throat will not be slit, your daughter will not be raped, and your house will not be set on fire. (We expect governments to do more than that—for example, to provide for us when we are old and sick—but we are speaking now of minimum requirements.) By safeguarding your life and property, the state grants you the freedom to pursue happiness.

Bentham called this freedom *security,* and he believed that without it no one could be happy. But freedom has its limits; the state neither forces you to pursue happiness (you are free to be unhappy) nor dictates which actions will help you to find it (you must determine that for yourself). Each person, as Bentham said, must "direct his own conduct to the production of his own happiness."[6] The state contributes to that endeavor by making sure that nothing obstructs you on your journey, so to speak. But what that journey entails—choices you make, actions you undertake, relationships you form, goals you set—is for you to decide. The government will intervene only if your pursuit of happiness obstructs someone else's. This is called *probity*: the state uses punishment, both threatened and actual, to stop us from harming each other, from making each other unhappy. (Which is one way of explaining bans on smoking in restaurants and bars.)

Now we see more clearly why Bentham's treatise on happiness is really a handbook of crime and punishment: because crime (more than anything else) diminishes our happiness, and punishment (more than anything else) guarantees the security that is its foundation. No one can be happy living in fear. Perverse as it seems, only by implementing a rational system of coercion—throwing people into jail—can the state promote the happiness of its citizens. It feels good to know that the man who broke into your home and stole your laptop is now off the streets and behind bars. Bentham was convinced that the loss of happiness (or its obverse, the creation of unhappiness) was the sole basis for punishing criminals. The more a crime "disturbs" happiness, he believed, the more "demand it creates for punishment."[7] Thus, a man who steals $100 from a poor person deserves a harsher sentence than a man who steals the same from a rich person because he has inflicted comparatively greater misery on his impecunious victim. He has, in effect, stolen *more* happiness.

Roadblocks to Happiness

Bentham makes a winning first impression. Staunch rationalists that we are, and believers in scientific inquiry, we probably approve of such a comprehensive approach to the good life. Utilitarianism teaches us that all people in all circumstances can determine—indeed, bring about—their own happiness.

But when we take a closer look, the flaws in Bentham's theory of happiness start to appear. Suddenly, there are wrinkles, creases, and gray hairs that had escaped our notice in an earlier moment of infatuation. For starters, the felicific calculus, no matter who uses it, does not work all that smoothly. It lacks units of measurement, and you cannot measure anything without a scale, whether inches and feet, ounces and pounds, or quarts and gallons. What, exactly, is the unit of measurement for happiness? The *happino*? Even if such a scale existed, it would be inadequate because no single unit of measurement can express both force and duration, which are the most basic aspects of how we feel our pleasures and pains. The pleasure of an orgasm is both intense and brief, but not intense-brief. The pleasure of reading a favorite novel is not moderate-long. We do not speak of pleasure in such a way. And yet, if we cannot calibrate differences of force and duration, then we cannot determine a final sum of happiness.

We may also come to doubt Bentham's view that pleasure is the sole and unerring basis of happiness. And that must be our gravest concern. Going back to his catalog of pleasure, we find something surprising: that "malevolence" appears as both a pain *and* a pleasure. How can this be? Surely, malevolence—wickedness, evildoing—must count only as a pain, because it entails suffering. True, Bentham would say, but that is only how the victim sees it. A malevolent person *enjoys* someone else's suffering, whether he or she inflicts it or merely rejoices at its occurrence. Pleasurable malevolence is not limited to archcriminals, for who does not quietly smile when an irritating colleague says something stupid in a meeting? In any act of malevolence, large or small, whatever pains the victim pleases the oppressor—and so creates happiness for the oppressor, if not for anyone else. Bentham does not shy away from that conclusion.

But we probably do shy away. Probably we want to condemn malevolent pleasures and deny that they could make anyone happy. But within the rules of Bentham's game—remember, all pleasures are created equal—we cannot make such a move. (Pushpin is as good as poetry.) Bentham gives us no rational basis for claiming that some pleasures are bad, even though our conscience tells us this must be so. That is an important insight about the pursuit of happiness: even if we embrace pleasure as the very substance and basis of a happy life, we feel that something *other* than pleasure must also be factored in. Mere pleasure cannot be the foundation of a worthy life. So although the attractions of utilitarian thought are undeniable—the logic, the clarity, the got-it-all-figured-out confidence—we must temper the attraction by recognizing that happiness has a dimension beyond pleasure, and this extra dimension—call it conscience, morality, or simply good character—must be given its due.

Is Everybody Happy?

It's not clear whether the greatest happiness principle guarantees that everyone will become happy. The confusion lies in the phrase itself. Initially, Bentham seems to have had in mind the overall amount of happiness—the *quantum,* as he called it—rather than its distribution within the community. This blunt quantum served an equally blunt purpose: to ensure that the majority enjoyed as much happiness as possible (and to hell with everybody else). Whether the majority was slim or overwhelming didn't matter, just as it didn't matter whether the minority was mildly discontent or in abject despair. The *only* thing that mattered was that the majority maximized its happiness.

In the happiness lottery—it's that random—we all stand an equal chance of winning. And the chances are pretty good, as more than 50 percent of us (the greatest number) will end up happy. But whereas most of us are guaranteed to win, some are bound to lose. We accept this disparity in outcome because the contest itself is fair: nobody has a head start, nobody is more likely to become happier than anyone else, and nobody can predict the outcome. As Bentham insisted, "Each [person] is to count for one and no one for more than one."[8] The tycoon and his tailor both have an equal claim to happiness. Utilitarianism thus satisfies our commitment to fair play, not because it guarantees equal outcomes (it doesn't) but because it ensures equal opportunities.

But fairness comes at a price, and that price is brutality. For most of us to be happy, some of us *must* be unhappy. These unhappy few may be woefully so, or even forced into slavery—whatever it takes for the majority to maximize its own happiness. This is the infamous "tyranny of the majority": the many are free to do whatever they want to the few, for example, not caring whether disabled people can board a bus or get inside their local library. (In *Democracy in America*, Alexis de Tocqueville warned that the systematic oppression of the minority by the majority was democracy's dark side.) Bentham, though no champion of individual moral rights, worried that his own principles might justify—worse, bring about—the oppression of the unhappy few by the happiness-hungry many.

Gradually, Bentham realized that the greater number of people must be prevented from tyrannizing the lesser number, even if this *lowered* the overall amount of happiness in the community. Toward the end of his career, in the late 1820s, he defended a more equitable distribution of happiness, which he called "the greatest happiness maximized." Inequities would be corrected by transferring some of the majority's happiness to the minority. That way, the happiness scales would be more balanced, and *everyone's* happiness, not just the lucky lottery winners', would be secured. A little less money in some people's pockets, but a much better life for everybody overall.

No Longer Hopeless

If ever a child were raised to be the test case for Bentham's strict principles, it was the moral philosopher John Stuart Mill (1806–1873). His father, James, a utilitarian and political radical, groomed his son from an early age for the commanding role he was to play in nineteenth-century Britain's intellectual life. The precocious seven-year-old read Plato's dialogues—in the original Greek. A year or two later, having mastered Latin, he took on Virgil, Horace, Livy, and Ovid. As an adolescent he turned to the study of natural sciences and law, reading Isaac Newton and Adam Smith.

Forbidden to attend university (although hardly short on knowledge), Mill took up a post at the East India Company alongside his father, who had secured the boy's appointment on the day after his seventeenth birthday. He eventually rose to the high-level position of chief examiner, and remained at the company until it was dissolved in 1858. In those days, when it took months for dispatches to arrive on steamships from Bombay, there wasn't much to occupy a clerk's time in the Office of the Examiner of India Correspondence. So Mill was free to devote half the day to his own, more voluminous writings—or, as he called them, his "private intellectual pursuits."[9]

At first, the young Mill was an ardent disciple of utilitarianism, praising it as the "keystone which held together the detached and fragmentary component parts of my knowledge."[10] For eighteen months he served as Bentham's secretary and struggled to transcribe the great man's rambling pronouncements. All that changed in 1827, when, barely out of his teens, Mill suffered what he called a "crisis in his mental history." We would call it a nervous breakdown. He complained of a "dull state of nerves" that made him "unsusceptible to enjoyment or pleasurable excitement." The company of friends gave him no joy and the privacy of books no relief. He could only stand by and watch as the "whole foundation on which [his] life was constructed fell down."[11] We ourselves may have never experienced such deep trauma, but who among us has not felt at one time or another a terrifying blankness of life, an emptiness on the inside?

Mill's turnaround came suddenly, as these things often do, when he was reading Jean-François Marmontel's *Mémoires*. Coming to the passage where the youth Marmontel confronts the reality of his father's death, Mill, to his astonishment, took on the character's sorrow and began to weep. This from a man who knew nothing but discipline and drill, restriction and rote. The teardrops that moistened the pages of his book were the longed-for sign that he "was no longer hopeless," no longer an unfeeling "stone." As the gloomy clouds lifted, Mill rejoiced to discover that he still possessed "some of the material out of which all worth of character, and all capacity for happiness, are made."[12]

A generation and more of Freudian psychobiographers have had a field day with this story, reading it as a classic Oedipal narrative of the son's subconscious desire to kill his father. There is some truth in that, for Mill's severe depression must have stemmed partly from repressed hostility toward an overbearing and emotionally indifferent parent on whom he was psychologically dependent. (After his father's death, nine years later, Mill developed a permanent twitch in his right eye.) But that is not how Mill himself wrote about the episode in a work that does not lack for unembarrassed candor. Rather, he understood his crisis to be a turning point in his view of happiness.

Poetry did the turning. Some months later, when he read Wordsworth for the first time, Mill finally liberated himself from the "reasoning machine" of Bentham's coldhearted logic. Enraptured by Wordsworth's evocations of nature and nature's beauty, Mill looked on poetry as "medicine for [his] state of mind" because it imparted to him "the perennial sources of happiness, when all the greater evils of life shall have been removed."[13] With those hopeful words, Mill ga to the story of his life a familiar Romantic theme: the triumph of imagination over reason. Reason, because it breaks things down into parts, allows us to understand their structure; but imagination, because it integrates, allows us to grasp their meaning. And it was meaning that Mill was after.

Embracing poetical culture—and its openness to emotion—led Mill to revise his view of happiness. Like Bentham, he continued to believe that happiness was the ultimate purpose of life and that it was bound up in pleasure and pleasurable experiences. But he formed a different idea about how to achieve it. The secret of happiness, he realized, was the paradox that you find it only by searching for something else. Happy people are those "who have their minds fixed on some object other than their own happiness; on the happiness of others, on the improvement of mankind, even on some art or pursuit, followed not as a means, but as itself an ideal end. Aiming thus at something else, they find happiness by the way."[14]

Rescuing Happiness

This was like throwing cold water over Bentham's head. In claiming that we find happiness indirectly, "by the way," Mill was explicitly rejecting Bentham's mechanistic view of human nature. Utility may well be the primary motive for all human behavior (we do all seek pleasure), but human beings cannot be reduced to machines that make rational—and *only* rational—calculations about it. There are "many things," Mill wrote, "which [utilitarian] doctrine . . . ought to have made room for, and did not." There is something within us that exceeds reason, escapes logic, and Mill faulted Bentham for neglecting this "many-sided" nature of human life.[15] We, too, might fault Bentham, for there is something undeniably cheerless and lonely about his rules and his catalogs and his felicific calculations. And disappointingly so: What should be more heartfelt than your pursuit of happiness? We do not want to live our lives according to textbook rules.

Yet Mill himself was the product of textbook rules, for the art of life had been categorically excluded from the highly regimented and solitary education that he had received from his father. (Horseback riding and hiking, yes, but other than scraps from Shakespeare, no poetry.) The exclusion had unfortunate consequences, as it put beyond the boy's reach all the feelings, experiences, and attitudes that, as a man, he understood to be the very heart of a life that was worthwhile. This is where Mill began to reshape the utilitarian idea of happiness and rescued it from being nothing more than a cold arithmetic fact: the ratio of pleasure to pain.

Happiness demands that we develop a "sense of honour," a "love of beauty," and a "love of order," Mill said.[16] The ultimate purpose of life is not to make blunt calculations of utility but to become a better person. (Though it sounds modern to say that happiness is related to self-improvement, it's actually one of the oldest ideas in Western culture, dating back to Aristotle, who taught that we "grow" into happiness like a sapling that grows into a tree.) Even as Mill acknowledged that the controlling environment of his youth had stunted his character development, he insisted that no person was a prisoner to his or her upbringing. With effort, *anyone* could alter his or her character for the better, and education's purpose was to make the betterment happen. As Mill knew firsthand from the therapeutic power of Wordsworth's poetry, aesthetic education provides one excellent opportunity for self-improvement. But learning a lesson from poetry requires imagination, the very thing that Bentham had so prejudicially cast aside.

In coming around to this view, Mill set himself the challenge of uniting the utilitarian pursuit of happiness-through-pleasure with a classical concern for the good life. Somehow, he had to show that maximizing utility was the right way to become a *better* person and not just a person who enjoyed more pleasure for pleasure's sake. The cornerstone of this new argument was the recognition that pleasures differed in *quality* as well as *quantity*. Some pleasures are better than others, and the better ones are those we should pursue, those that will make us truly happy.

Pigs and Fools and the Quality of Pleasure

"It is quite compatible with the principle of utility," wrote Mill, "to recognise the fact, that some kinds of pleasure are more desirable and more valuable than others." It is "absurd," he continued in his famous essay *Utilitarianism* (1861), to suppose that the "estimation of pleasures" should depend on "quantity alone."[17] But how do we tell higher pleasures from lower ones? Partly by who experiences them. The lowest pleasures—food, drink, defecation, and sex—entail mere physical sensation, and so are experienced by humans and animals alike. The highest pleasures—reason, imagination, and moral sentiment—rely on thought, and so are enjoyed only by humans. Moreover, we deem lower pleasures inferior because they are short-lived and require neither effort nor skill (a hungry person does not need to be taught the pleasure of eating). By contrast, higher pleasures are more enduring and do require effort and skill (we need to be taught how to play a Beethoven sonata). So the way to be happy is to pick our pleasures carefully.

We prize the highest pleasures precisely because they involve uniquely human faculties, and thus are the sign and testament of our superior place in nature's hierarchy. The more a pleasure is exclusively human, said Mill, the higher it is, and the more assiduously we should pursue it. This is a familiar argument—"Go for the gold," as the modern Olympians cry—and one that appeals to the vanity of our species. For us, nothing but the best. As rational actors, we know that the best pleasures are intellectual, not sensual, and so we privilege the mind over the body.

But make no mistake: no puritans are we. To aim exclusively for high intellectual pleasures is no hardship, no sacrifice of something more enjoyable, Mill argues, because no one "really wish[es] to sink into what he feels to be a lower grade of existence."[18] If we *did* wish to slide into a debased form of life, then we would no longer be human; we would be animals. But we are not animals, not any more. Having broken through the evolutionary ceiling, we are not about to fall back down, especially when it has taken so many thousands of generations to get to where we now are.

When Mill's contemporary, the historian Thomas Carlyle, denounced utilitarianism as a "pig philosophy," he meant that its emphasis on pleasure reduced human beings to the base level of animals. If happiness entails only the gratification of desire, Carlyle warned, then happiness is hardly worth having. Rolling in mud and sticking your snout in a trough cannot possibly count as living the good life. Unless, of course, you are a pig—and then it is very good indeed.

The flaw in Carlyle's argument, at least from Mill's perspective, is his assumption that humans and pigs enjoy the same pleasures. That is true, but only partially so. All creatures go forth and multiply, but only we humans compose sonnets and paint pictures about it. Thus, in his memorable riposte to Carlyle, Mill declared, "It is better to be a human being dissatisfied than a pig satisfied; better to be Socrates dissatisfied than a fool satisfied. And if the fool, or the pig, is of a different opinion, it is because they only know their own side of the question. The other party to the comparison knows both sides."[19]

In others words, pigs and fools don't know what they're missing. Which is what makes them pigs and fools in the first place. But we who are wise, we who know "both sides" of the question, can distinguish piggy pleasures from Socratic ones. What makes one pleasure superior to another is the "nobleness of character"—courage, nobility, dignity, duty, or self-sacrifice—that it demands. These virtues are what really matter about pleasure and are the very reason we pursue it: to possess its desirable attributes so that we might acquire a noble character.

The Daisy Chain of Happiness

Eager to prove that the utilitarian vision of happiness was altruistic, not selfish, Mill tried to reconcile the seemingly incompatible goals of the individual (what *I* want) and the group (what *they* want). His resolution was mutuality: your happiness depends on mine. And not just mine, but everyone else's. Thus, you cannot be happy unless your neighbors are, just as they cannot be unless you are. True, we are still motivated by the desire to maximize our own happiness, but we come to realize that this desire can be fulfilled only indirectly. If you look after someone else, someone else will look after you, and everyone will look after each other in a daisy chain of happiness. And if a person of noble character is not always the happier for his or her nobility, "there can be no doubt that it makes other people happier, and that the world in general is immensely a gainer by it."[20]

We must secure other people's happiness first, because that is the only way to guarantee ours, and we must look on ourselves as a "disinterested and benevolent spectator." From this new, detached perspective, we see that our desires are no more important, no more urgent, than anyone else's. No greater necessity attaches itself to your happiness than to mine, and so you will always treat me with the same care and concern that you would naturally bestow on yourself. So whole-heartedly did Mill believe that utilitarian ethics required total regard for others that he compared it, unabashedly (outrageously, some might say), to Christianity: "In the golden rule of Jesus of Nazareth, we read the complete spirit of the ethics of utility. To do as one would be done by, and to love one's neighbour as oneself constitutes the ideal perfection of utilitarian morality."[21]

But let us not be so quick to preach. Suppose that in your moment of ideal perfection, you sacrifice your happiness for mine. Remember, your sacrifice is not good in itself—virtue is *not* its own reward—but good only to the extent that it makes you happy (and, as a bonus, maybe a few others, too). Not exactly selfless, your sacrifice is a rationally calculated investment—do not call it noble—which you expect will yield a high rate of return. If you thought otherwise you wouldn't make the investment. So, contrary to the gospel's spirit, your left hand *does* know what your right hand is doing. But results matter most. If your sacrifice makes other people happy, then it will have been worthwhile, because in the long run it will make you happy, too. But if it fails, if no one becomes happier, then your efforts will have been "wasted" (that's Mill's word), and you would have been better off just looking after yourself—and yourself alone.[22]

Resist the Dark Side

Why do so many of us find utilitarianism morally repugnant? After all, it aims to make most people happy. Yet we already know the objections: people can derive happiness (in principle) from actions that most of us regard as immoral; the majority is free to tyrannize the minority; and individual moral rights are left unprotected. Utilitarianism makes you pay a staggeringly high price for your happiness.

The rigidity of Bentham's scheme troubled Mill, who tried to overcome it by appealing to "the art of life" and the "nobleness of character" that have nothing to do with maximizing pleasure. In effect, he made something other than pleasure the basis for action, and so made a distinction between things we *do* and things we *should do*. He was, in effect, saying, We should seek pleasure not for itself, but only for some particular aspect of it that we regard as valuable. Mill had to follow this curved line of reasoning because otherwise he could not have claimed, as he did, that a small quantity of a higher pleasure (say, a few minutes reading Wordsworth) counts for more than a large quantity of a lower pleasure (say, a few hours at the all-you-can-eat buffet). This may be a quibble of interest only to philosophers, but there is a point of direct concern for us: that pleasure may well be the basis of happiness, but never in an extreme way, and never when divorced from our sense of what a good and purposeful life means.

2

PLEASURE IS GOOD
(THE EPICUREANS)

Plato had been dead for seven years when Epicurus (341–271 B.C.) was born in an Athenian colony on the island of Samos in the Aegean Sea. The son of a schoolmaster, he became interested in philosophy as an adolescent. He first journeyed to Athens in 323 B.C. to begin his military service. Upon its completion he rejoined his family, by then relocated to Colophon in Asia Minor after the conquering Macedonians had expelled the Athenian colonists from Samos. For the next decade Epicurus continued to study philosophy. In 311 B.C., age thirty, he began teaching in Mytilene, and left soon afterward for Lampsacus. Five years later he returned to Athens, where he taught for the remaining thirty-five years of his life.

Epicurus preached his radical philosophy at a time when Athens's grand democratic ideals had been jeopardized by despotism and civic unrest. Popular religion inspired not faith, but bewilderment and terror. Plato and Aristotle, the great philosophers of the century that had just passed, no longer seemed relevant. In that troubling moment, succumbing to skepticism and despair seemed the easy way out. For anyone disenchanted with the way of the world, yet still committed to leading the good life, the highly self-sufficient philosophy of

Epicurus—to be happy, just seek pleasure—must have been powerfully seductive.

At no time was the seduction more powerful than at the end of Epicurus's own life. Unlike Socrates, Epicurus died of natural causes (kidney failure), but like his philosophical forebear, he drew his last breath surrounded by friends and followers. After climbing into a bronze tub filled with hot water, Epicurus drank a glass of wine, instructed his pupils to remember his teachings, and then peacefully drifted into unconsciousness. In the weeks prior to his death he had suffered agonizing pain from kidney stones. Yet he insisted that he would die a blessed and happy man because his thoughts remained fixed on the joyful memory of conversations with friends. The over-, powering pleasure that Epicurus derived from these memories, so he claimed, rendered him insensitive to pain. Cicero, writing two hundred years later, dismissed this as mere fustian: no memory, however ecstatic, can prevent anyone from feeling pain. A man exposed to unbearable heat does not comfort himself by remembering that he once took a cool bath.

We can never know whether Epicurus exaggerated on his deathbed. But we *do* know that with his dying words he imparted what he believed was the secret of happiness: storing up pleasures against rainy days of pain.

Philosophy (and Other Things) in a Garden

Disaffected Athenians found themselves drawn to Epicurus because of his freethinking view that *everyone* could benefit from philosophy. "Let no one," he exhorted, "delay the study of philosophy while young nor weary of it when old. For no one is either too young or too old for the health of the soul."[1] Epicureans regarded philosophy as something of a team sport, and so they did it in groups; indeed, many of them lived in communes modeled on the one just outside Athens, called "the Garden," that the philosopher himself had established.

In this secret garden lived both men and women, both free and slave. That servants and women enjoyed the same status as freemen made these communities socially reformist. But not collectivist: everyone retained private possessions because Epicurus believed that holding property in common implied that the members of the community mistrusted each other. Still, income was redistributed, for the wealthier residents were expected to help finance the enterprise, which included copying and publishing Epicurean handbooks.

Partly because the community dared to include women (including those shady dames Baby Lion, Little Conquest, and Tits) and partly because it was cut off from the Athenian city-state, outsiders grew suspicious of this philosophical cult and its charismatic founder. Epicurus stood accused of being a hypocrite who perpetrated the very vices that he condemned. Timocrates, a disgruntled former student, claimed that Epicurus vomited twice a day because he consumed so many extravagant foods. More damning, it was rumored that orgies were held in the garden. The slanderous charges gained such credibility that Diogenes Laertius, writing some six hundred years after the fact, repeated them in his *Lives and Sayings of Famous Philosophers*. Much like a modern tabloid journalist, Diogenes started with the sensational aspect of the story: rumors of sexual depravity and accusations of indecent conduct. Only later, after his readers had been sufficiently titillated, did he bother to admit that the lurid allegations made against Epicurus were, in fact, false, and that the philosopher's moral character remained beyond reproach.

Tokens of Thought

In the ancient world, you would have encountered philosophy in the shape of proverbs and open letters. Once memorized, a proverb could be called to mind in an anxious moment. Letters gained a wide audience because they were passed from hand to hand and read aloud to those who could not read. If you required a reassuringly material form of wisdom, you might inscribe a helpful proverb onto a picture frame or a favorite piece of jewelry. Sometimes words were unnecessary. A statue of Epicurus, his portrait, or even his likeness carved on a signet ring: all could inspire deep thoughts in a believer. Far from being devoid of meaning, such objects served as tangible and encouraging reminders that wisdom lies within everyone's reach. For his more ambitious followers, Epicurus composed letters outlining the basic principles of his beliefs. These letters were not private correspondence but public documents; they were shared, copied, and circulated, much like the letters of St. Paul to the early Christians. And for the diehards willing to undertake intensive study, Epicurus wrote out his arguments in lengthy treatises.

Ranging from the simple to the complex, these varied forms of philosophical knowledge demanded of their users correspondingly varied levels of mental effort. But no one should sneer at the low-end products hawked in the marketplace of ideas in the classical world, nor be driven by status anxiety to covet only the high-end ones. The crucial thing was not that you should progress from the easy to the difficult—from wearing lucky charms to reading lengthy treatises—but that you should find your own level. Whether carved in marble, set in gold, or written on papyrus, philosophical knowledge was a valuable commodity never in short supply. The many and diverse tokens of Epicurean thought that circulated in the ancient world made the philosophical life available to anyone who wanted it, and in a way that made sense to them. For what good is a way of thinking about life that does not make sense?

Appropriately for someone who believed that ideas matter to all, Epicurus was a staggeringly prolific writer of philosophical and scientific treatises. His greatest work, *On Nature*, filled thirty-seven volumes (scrolls, actually; the book had yet to be invented), of which all that remain are some papyrus fragments excavated at Herculaneum, the Roman town destroyed along with Pompeii when Mount Vesuvius erupted in A.D. 79. Discovered only in 1928, the fragments of this monumental work rested undisturbed for nearly nineteen hundred years. Of other works we know only the titles: *On Love, On Religion, On Fate,* and *On Music*.

The only works of Epicurus that have been preserved in their entirety are three letters: the Letter to Herodotus is the simplified account of his philosophy written for beginners; the Letter to Pythocles, on astronomy and meteorology, was probably written not by Epicurus himself but by one of his followers; and the Letter to Menoeceus, to which we will soon turn, sets out his views on happiness. Also surviving are two collections of short epigrammatic texts known as the Principal Doctrines and the Vatican Sayings. They consist of the proverbs that Epicureans once memorized and recited, and thus give us a fair idea of what the man himself originally taught about the good life.

The Four Principles of Happiness

When Epicurus wrote to his friend Menoeceus about happiness, he focused on the core elements that would be present in the life of *any* happy person. It never entered his mind to offer Menoeceus (or anybody else) advice on what to do in this or that situation. (Unlike the ancients, we expect, lazily, that theories of happiness will provide instant solutions to life's most intractable problems.) Epicurus emphasized that being happy meant subscribing to four fundamental principles:

- The gods exist, but not in the way we suppose.
- Death is nothing to fear.
- Pleasure is the key to happiness.
- Everything we need to be happy is easy to obtain.

A happy person, says Epicurus, is someone who has correct beliefs about the gods, faces death without fear, pursues pleasure (but, as we shall see, in a highly qualified way), and recognizes the value of prudence and simplicity. If we live by these values we will act wisely, so that we move closer to happiness; if not, then we will act unwisely—and thus bring unhappiness upon ourselves. In either case, our actions are undertaken not in accordance with preexisting rules or commandments (thou shalt, thou shalt not) but in accordance with our own appraisal of the quality of our life as a whole.

The gods exist, but not in the way we suppose.

Despite claims made by his detractors to the contrary, Epicurus taught that divine beings do exist and that we can possess clear knowledge of them. Yet he also taught that many of us hold false beliefs about the nature of the gods. Our mistake is to attribute to them traits that actually diminish or distort their perfection. Many ancient Greeks believed that the gods watched over them, took an interest in their affairs, rewarded them for worship, and punished them for neglect. In short, they believed that the gods behaved just as they did. Wrong, said Epicurus: the gods do not behave just like us for the simple, yet frequently ignored reason that they are *not* just like us.

The gods exist in a state of perpetual bliss (that is part of what makes them gods) and so remain untroubled by all that transpires in the world beneath them. "Nothing cankers their peace of mind," as the tormented Roman poet Lucretius enviously observed.[2] (According to legend, he killed himself after being driven mad by a love potion that his neglected wife, Lucilla, had slipped into his drink.) Because deities need nothing to fulfill their desires, they have no cause to intervene in our lives; in fact, they bear no responsibility for creating our planet and sustaining the life forms, including us, that inhabit it. In Epicurean cosmology the earth exists only as the accidental result of atoms colliding into each other as they move randomly throughout the universe.

Today, we are bound to find this a rather godless view of God: If he did not create the world and if he does not love us, then why bother worshipping him? Why, indeed, Epicurus would reply. Happiness begins, he would go on to say, with the realization—initially unnerving, but then liberating—that the gods do not condescend to involve themselves in our affairs. To believe otherwise is to deny ourselves any chance of happiness. For when we worry that the gods are going to punish us, we succeed only in making ourselves miserable. And you don't have to be an ancient Greek to believe, as many people do today, that humanity's hard-won freedom is freedom from the superstitious fear of God.

Death is nothing to fear.

Though widespread, the fear of death is irrational and absurd. To fear something (being diagnosed with cancer, losing your pension) means that we think its consequences are bad; to desire something (a clean bill of health, financial security) means we think its consequences are good. Yet to know whether something is good or bad, Epicurus believed, we must first experience it, directly or vicariously. (Children know—*really* know—that it is bad to touch a hot stove only after burning their fingers doing it.) Death, however, is something that we can never experience because it is nothing other than the *end* of experience. We will all undergo the experience of dying, as Epicurus acknowledged; but that is not the same as being dead. Nor can we contact the departed to find out what being dead is like. Thus, we can never be in a legitimate position to call death good or bad. And if we cannot call death bad, then we cannot rationally fear it. If we do, our fears are groundless. "Death is nothing to us," Epicurus taught. "When we exist, death is not yet present, and when death is present, then we do not exist."[3] For both the quick and the dead, death is irrelevant.

Moreover, the fear of death is absurd, because it leads us to feel pain about something that has not yet happened—and something that may not be painful when it does happen. Only a fool, Epicurus contends, would fear the *prospect* of death. Those who fear death because they believe the gods will punish them in the afterlife spend this life frightened that they will suffer the everlasting torments of hell. Others fear death because they are convinced there is no afterlife. Saddened by the possibility of oblivion, they mourn their own death prematurely. All this worry and anxiety and brooding cause a great deal of harm, Epicurus warned, because they distract us from the very things that are necessary for our happiness. We traumatize ourselves with the threat of eternal damnation and depress ourselves with the thought that we do not possess an immortal soul. All too easily, death casts a pall over life.

Epicurus is telling us that in this world we are fundamentally free: there are no gods who once created us, now watch over us, and will punish us either in this life or the next. Indeed, there is no afterlife, at least not one that we can experience in any immediate way. Released from the ancient bonds of superstition, whether a mistaken belief about the gods or an irrational fear of death, we find that happiness is possible in our earthly state of complete freedom. Instead of worrying about punishment in the next world, we should try to eliminate the anxiety we feel in *this* world. Stay focused on the here and now. That way happiness lies.

Pleasure is the key to happiness.

We seek pleasure, but we may not do just as we please. Not because there is an absolute moral framework for judging actions (no such thing exists, said Epicurus) but because we realize that some actions will increase our happiness and others diminish it. For Epicurus, the correct standard for judging actions is not whether they conform to a moral code, but whether they make us feel tranquil—that is, free from anxiety. How else would we judge them? Our rational self-interest tells us that we should perform an action if it is pleasurable and refrain if it is not. Nowadays, we are likely to think of reason and pleasure as opposites: the mind's controlling force declares war on the body's unbridled passions. But Epicurus did not think that way at all; for him, reason and pleasure walk hand in hand.

How can we know with certainty whether a particular action leads to tranquility or anxiety? If we can't be certain, then we have no option but to act randomly, learn from hard experience, and hope for the best result. That is a dangerously inefficient way to live, for there is no guarantee that we will make the right decision. We must be certain. Epicurus anticipated as much, for he declared that we *can* know which actions will (or won't) promote our happiness—once we learn to distinguish between necessary and unnecessary desires. We will be able to identify the desires that deserve to be satisfied, those that should be deferred, and those that must be renounced.

Our deliberations will not be overly complex, Epicurus predicted, because there are only three kinds of desires: natural and necessary (those that liberate us from pain); natural but unnecessary (those that liberate us from pain but may cause harm); and unnatural and unnecessary (those that do not liberate us from pain and may cause harm). No desire can be unnatural *and* necessary because those terms are mutually exclusive. We embrace a desire to the extent that it leads toward the tranquility in which happiness consists, and we resist it to the extent that it leads away from tranquility. Thus, we *must* satisfy desires that are natural and necessary because they are vital to our happiness. We *may* satisfy desires that are natural but unnecessary, as long as they cause us no harm. And we *should never* satisfy desires that are unnatural and unnecessary because they are never conducive to happiness.

Everything we need to be
happy is easy to obtain.

It is easy to obtain all things necessary for our happiness and difficult to obtain all things unnecessary for it. Luxurious versions of basic things—Prada shoes, a Bentley, a villa in Tuscany—require time and money not just to acquire but also to maintain. We enjoy such luxuries (who wouldn't?), but we must not, Epicurus warned, become dependent on them. Being greedy, wanting more than we need, will only reduce our chance of happiness. If we crave luxuries, then it will become harder and harder to be satisfied. No shoes will be stylish enough, no car fast enough, no house palatial enough.

Our own experience tells us this all the time: that the pleasure we derive from any object gradually declines as we get used to it. The charming scientific name for this process is "hedonic adaptation": the moment we get used to something nice, it stops feeling nice. Buying a new car is the classic example of becoming habituated to an object of desire. At first, your expensive Jaguar gives you a great deal of enjoyment. But sooner or later, it won't seem any more attractive than the less expensive Volvo that it replaced. And so you start fantasizing about your next car, in an unstoppable, but forlorn hope that *it* will be the one to completely satisfy your desire. Of course it won't—because in the chain of desire, there is no last link.

Many of us today are trapped in a spiral of consumption that compels us to buy ever more extravagant items to maintain a consistent amount of pleasure. At some point, and it arrives sooner and sooner, pleasure turns first to boredom, then to dissatisfaction, and, finally, to anxiety. We torture ourselves by asking why our hard-earned possessions fail to make us happy. The persistence of unsatisfied desire is a theme that arises in many philosophies of happiness, both Eastern and Western. It is a truth universally acknowledged that luxuries never make us truly content because they satisfy our desires only temporarily.

So the secret of happiness is to attain the state of tranquility in which we no longer need to satisfy any desire, no longer need to pursue any pleasure. This is a secret easily unraveled. We seek pleasure only when we are in pain. If we are no longer in pain (for that is what it means to be tranquil), then we will no longer seek pleasure. Thus, we make decisions about desire—indulge this one, defer that one, suppress yet another—not in terms of the desire itself, but in terms of what is good for our life as a whole.

This broader perspective stops us from being profligate in our quest for pleasure. In a sober frame of mind, we will think clearly and carefully about how best to reduce the turmoil in our souls. We will find that simple things yield as much pleasure as luxuries do. And once we grow accustomed to simple things we will have a better time in life because we will appreciate luxuries all the more when, or if, they come along. (This is a good argument for not spoiling your children: leave them something to look forward to as they grow up.) "Those who least need extravagance enjoy it most," was Epicurus's home truth.[4]

All of the Pleasure, None of the Guilt

Many of us will find it puzzling that Epicurus unites pleasure and virtue, especially if our heritage is Judeo-Christian or Islamic, for we might well have been taught that pleasure and virtue exist in inverse proportion: the more pleasure we feel, the less virtuous we become. Hence the phrase "guilty pleasures." Such an expression would have been meaningless to Epicurus, who found nothing illicit in the desire for pleasure.

For Epicureans, pleasure is the *sole* motive for action because it is the only standard for judging the rightness of conduct. An act is moral if it produces more pleasure than pain, immoral if it produces more pain than pleasure. So when making ethical judgements, you should consider neither the action itself (Is it right to do *x*?), nor its consequences for others (If I do *x*, what will happen?), but only the *emotions* that it will arouse within you (If I do *x*, will it make me feel good?). Plainly this is a relative, not an absolute, standard. The same act, when performed by different people, or by the same person under different circumstances, can be both moral, if it brings pleasure, and immoral, if it brings pain. Sex with your spouse can be a wonderfully satisfying expression of your love, whereas sex with your mistress can make you feel guilty for having broken your marriage vows and anxious that you'll be discovered.

Within this closed system, virtue—the disposition to act morally—is not an end in itself, but a means to pleasure. We are virtuous not because we like virtue (or at least not necessarily) but because we like the pleasure that comes from it. It is impossible, then, for an Epicurean to imagine a virtue that does not automatically entail pleasure. Virtue will not reside in one fixed place because many different actions can be virtuous. Yet wherever virtue is found, pleasure will also be there. And happiness, too.

In his dialogue *On the Ends of Goods and Evils,* Cicero provided an instructive example of how virtue and pleasure always turn up together. The virtuous man will be courageous, Cicero explained, not because he esteems courage but because he desires to live without anxiety. And exhibiting courage is a highly effective way to have an anxiety-free life. Similarly, the virtuous man is temperate not because he values temperance, but because he values the peace of mind that it begets. For the ancient Greeks and Romans, temperance was a broad character trait: the strength to act moderately in all types of situations. It meant far more than our narrow modern sense of merely abstaining from alcohol. Today, we might call it being responsible, mature, or level-headed.

Still, we can use the familiar scenario of knowing your limit. Let's say that you prefer not to be hung over on Sunday morning, and so you make sure that you don't get drunk on Saturday night. Epicurus would say that makes you virtuous (you stay in command of your faculties, which is the virtue of temperance) and therefore happy. But remember: you acted that way not to be virtuous but to have pleasure (in this case, the pleasure of not suffering from cottonmouth and a headache). Yet in obtaining that pleasure you found that you were also being virtuous. You found that you were happy.

It Hurts So Good

A happy life is not simply one in which at any moment pleasure outweighs pain. All pleasures are good, but not all should be pursued; all pains are bad, but not all should be avoided. As Epicurus taught, we must choose our pleasures and pains judiciously. It is wisdom to understand that sometimes we reject pleasure and accept pain in order to secure a greater, more lasting pleasure.

By stopping himself from getting drunk, the temperate man wins for himself a higher pleasure (tranquility) by renouncing a lower one (inebriation). The intemperate man, however, chases after—and obtains—modest pleasures, but then he also suffers vastly disproportionate pains: disease, poverty, disgrace, and, finally, imprisonment. All that from one too many glasses of wine. Cicero used this extreme example to make the general point that the single-minded pursuit of pleasure is not always our best course of action.

Not that we need Cicero to tell us that, because we make pleasure-pain calculations every single day. Not all of them are high-minded. Many people pay to do something in their leisure time that they probably avoid doing at home or in the office: raising and lowering heavy objects. Although painful and boring, working out does yield pleasurable results: greater strength, increased energy, and a dramatically improved ability to attract similarly strong and energetic sexual partners. Surely all these pleasures are worth a little pain. (There's a chain of fitness clubs in Washington, DC, called Results, an establishment whose very name exhorts its body-conscious clientele to discount immediate pains and focus on promised glories.) If you have ever invoked the mantra "No pain, no gain" beloved of fitness freaks everywhere, then Epicurus would be proud of you (after all, the ancient Greeks invented gym culture), but he would also think that you could find better things to do with your time than building up your biceps.

Sometimes, it's best to renounce pleasure. An increasing number of teenagers from families on the religious right have publicly sworn to abstain from premarital sex because they believe that "true love waits." (A recent television documentary featured "Texas teenage virgins" taking just this kind of "purity pledge.") Epicurus would have mixed feelings about voluntary abstinence. He would reject outright the religious motive—on the grounds that there is no God who dictates moral standards—but would admire the restraint. Yet the larger point he would make to the purity pledge-takers is that wise people behave prudently, not recklessly; they forsake pleasure and endure pain *only* when those sacrifices enable them to enjoy greater pleasure or to avoid greater pain. In itself, the sacrifice is meaningless. So if you're going to renounce pleasure, you'd better have a compelling reason; otherwise, there's no point. You're just being false to your own nature.

No matter how much pain we suffer, our pleasure—if it is of the highest sort—remains undiminished. And if our pleasure is undiminished, then so, too, is our happiness. It was for this reason—because the highest pleasures are indestructible—that Epicurus claimed that a wise person would remain happy even while being tortured. (The type of person Epicurus had in mind was an innocent victim, not someone who deserved punishment.) This is a bizarre claim for anyone to make, but especially bizarre for someone who believes that pleasure is the root of all happiness. Leaving aside sadomasochistic rituals practiced by consenting adults, surely no pleasure can arise from torture. So how can the wise man remain happy while pain is inflicted on him?

No contradiction arises, Epicurus declared, for a reason that we have already seen. In all circumstances, and especially an extreme circumstance like torture, the wise person focuses neither on the activity (being pistol-whipped or prodded with a live wire) nor its consequences (unbearable pain), but on his *attitude* toward the activity (its inability to overpower his happiness). Once a person is already happy, neither accident nor misfortune, neither calamity nor injury, can diminish his happiness. Because happiness is a pronouncement on one's life as a whole—and thus detached from any particular episode or experience—it cannot be dislodged by a single moment of suffering, no matter how intense. Such reasoning might strike us as ludicrous: no one can be happy while being tortured; it is the very opposite of happiness. But Epicurus's reasoning starts to look more persuasive once you begin to see happiness from a different angle: not as a feeling, but as a disposition of character.

Because the proper pursuit of pleasure is not about thrill seeking, not about living for the moment, our ultimate goal cannot be to experience as many different pleasures as possible. Rather, it must be to achieve the state of tranquility in which we feel no pain. Indeed, the greatest pleasure, insisted Epicurus, arises from the complete absence of pain. When you experience the lack of any desire that needs to be fulfilled, you find yourself in a state of pleasurable tranquility; nothing convulses you, nothing disquiets you.

Such pleasures will vary in kind (because they will have different causes) but never in degree, for there is a totality to the absence of pain that cannot be qualified. When pain is absent it is completely so, and the resulting pleasure is similarly complete because nothing stands in its way. The highest pleasures are perfect, and like perfection they can be neither measured nor quantified; they are all or nothing, with no in between. It is impossible, then, for these pleasures to be made more intense because they can exist only in maximum intensity. Thus, although Epicurus spoke of attaining happiness, he did not speak (like Bentham) of maximizing it, as if someone could acquire *more* happiness by behaving differently. To attain true happiness means that you've already, as they say, maxed out.

This makes for a nice theory, but does it work in practice? Does anyone actually experience pleasure in the absence of pain? Imagine a man, tired and thirsty, wandering in the desert. On the point of collapse, he finally reaches an oasis with cool, clear water. What will give him the most pleasure? A drink of water, surely. Not so, said Epicurus. The thirsty man's greatest pleasure lies not in having his thirst quenched but in no longer being thirsty. What our dehydrated wanderer really desires, according to Epicurus, is not the pleasure of drinking but the absence of the pain—parched throat and cracked, blistered lips—that makes him want to drink in the first place. The happy man is not he who drinks when thirsty but he who has no thirst. It's not that we want food, drink, and shelter (although that's certainly how we experience it) but that we want *not* to be hungry, *not* to be thirsty, *not* to be cold. We become truly happy not when we satisfy our desires but in the *next* moment: the moment when we realize that we have no desires left to satisfy.

Accentuate the Negative

Our intuitive understanding of pleasure—*feeling good*—is not one that Epicurus fully shared. Otherwise, he would not say things like "Not being thirsty is a great pleasure." The difference between Epicurus and us is that he believed in two distinct kinds of pleasure: positive and negative.

Positive pleasure depends on pain because it is nothing other than the *removal* of pain: you're thirsty, so you drink a glass of water. Negative pleasure, however, is the state of equilibrium in which you no longer feel pain and thus no longer need any (positive) pleasure to get rid of that pain: you're not thirsty, so you don't need that glass of water. Positive pleasures are *kinetic* because they imply activity: eating, drinking, dancing, having sex. Such pleasures seem actual or real because they entail direct sensory experience. In drinking a glass of water when thirsty I am actually doing something; moreover, I am doing something quantifiable: I can drink a little or a lot.

Negative pleasures, by contrast, are *static* because they imply inactivity: *not* eating because I am full, *not* drinking because my thirst is already quenched, *not* dancing because I have done it enough, *not* having sex because I am not aroused. Such pleasures seem nebulous because they do not entail direct sensory experience. Precisely because they arise from the lack of pain, they entail only indirect experience—that is, the pleasurable state of having no unfulfilled desires. This type of pleasure cannot be quantified, cannot be understood in terms of more and less. "How much are you not hungry?" is a nonsensical question.

Epicurus upheld the superiority of negative pleasures because he believed them to be total and complete. To be truly happy we should seek not the limited kinetic pleasure that comes from satisfying a particular desire but the boundless static pleasure—the absence of pain—that comes from having no desires that need satisfying in the first place. When every desire is fulfilled, then every pain will vanish and we will reach the very limit of all possible pleasure. Epicurus promised that in happiness we will rival Zeus himself. Positive pleasures we must regard as inferior because they are necessarily partial and incomplete: our clothes could always be more stylish, our meals more savory, our orgasms more volcanic. As long as we have such unfulfilled desires we will be in pain. In happiness, we will lag far behind Zeus.

Once we understand that Epicurus defined the highest pleasure negatively—the absence of pain—we can see how unfairly he has been judged not just by his contemporaries, but by posterity. Despite centuries of rumors to the contrary, Epicurus was no soft voluptuary. That much we know from his letter to Menoeceus: "When, therefore, we say that pleasure is the end, we do not mean the pleasures of the dissolute and those [pleasures] that lie in enjoyment, as some suppose who are ignorant and disagree with us or take it in a bad sense, but rather not being pained in body and not being troubled in soul."[5]

Whenever we call someone with a taste for fine wines and gourmet food an "epicure," we abuse the term. In truth, such people are degenerate epicures because they seek only to maximize positive pleasures. The genuine epicure, who prizes only negative pleasures, leads a spartan and ascetic existence. The strict logic of Epicurean ethics allows for nothing else: we are happy only when tranquil; we are tranquil only when free from pain; we are free from pain only when all desires are fulfilled; desires can be fulfilled only if they are moderate.

Correctly understood, Epicureanism is never a license for overindulgence, but always a pledge of austerity. Its ethical principles demand discipline and discernment. "How serious, how temperate, how austere," Cicero approvingly observed, "is the school that is supposed to be sensual, lax, and luxurious."[6] You will not lead a life worthy of happiness if you are wanton and licentious. Indeed, it is precisely the harsh side of Epicurean philosophy that explains why early Christian theologians recognized the merit of its strict ethics, even if they could not countenance its disavowal of God's presence in history.

In truth, being an epicure doesn't sound much like fun. Still, Epicurus maintained that the temperate man is happy because he has avoided the pains suffered by the intemperate man. For example, he takes pleasure in his sobriety, knowing that he is not hung over. But does that ring true? Can the mere absence of something, even something as distasteful as a hangover, be called a pleasure? It can barely be called an experience. The pleasure of waking up sober is a phantom pleasure. You can't really grasp it; and even if you could, it's far too bland to be enjoyable. You'd have to be a very particular kind of person—a recovering alcoholic, say—to feel that waking up sober is a great pleasure. And being a recovering alcoholic is a traumatically high price to pay for the pleasure of sobriety. Surely, if anybody is enjoying pleasure it's the *intemperate* man, for his pleasures are palpable: he can see, smell, and taste his whisky. True, if he drinks too deeply from the cup of pleasure he may repent the morning after, but the morning's pain cannot erase the pleasures of the night before.

But Epicurus insisted that negative pleasures are the only ones worth having. And yet the nagging problem is that negative pleasures don't look like pleasures, at least not the kind of pleasures that we're accustomed to having. If you think that Epicurus was inconsistent in how he defined pleasure, then you are thinking just like Cicero. He accused the Greek philosopher of intellectual sleight of hand, trying to make us believe that two different things—pleasure and pain—are one and the same.

Sneering at the Masses

Cicero was no knee-jerk critic. As a youth he attended lectures given by the Epicurean teacher Phaedrus. In the *Tusculan Disputations* he betrayed more sympathy for the Stoics, but he did give the Epicureans a fair shake. Ultimately, he rejected the philosophy of Epicurus because it relied too heavily on sensory data, exalted pleasure, precluded any possibility of divine intervention, and, most worrying of all for the great Roman statesman, it devalued public life. Cicero was convinced that anyone who practiced Epicurean teachings risked leading a life of sheer indolence, perhaps even debauchery. Anyone who, like Cicero, was committed to life in the civic arena would find little to satisfy them in Epicurus's renouncing spirit.

Cicero's reasons for doubting the Epicurean vision of happiness are his reasons, not ours. Many of us would not, for example, demand that happiness be open to the possibility of divine intervention. But one of Cicero's concerns we probably *do* share: the expectation that a happy life is connected to the world, not divorced from it. Part of being happy means that we are at home in the world as we find it.

But inside the walled garden on the outskirts of Athens the pupils of Epicurus learned a different lesson: that the good life meant being cut off from the business, and busyness, of the world outside. To desire what the world desires was to make the prospect of happiness even more remote. The values of public life—fame, respect, status, and wealth—were no values at all, and such insubstantial pleasures quickly faded. Worse, the statesman ran the risk of slander and defeat, and so his reputation was never secure. Such a life was too fragile a basis for lasting happiness. We would be much better off, Epicurus counseled, with a life of quiet contentment. And so the only option, if we truly want to achieve the state of tranquility necessary for happiness, is to withdraw from the world and limit our community to a few like-minded friends. That is why Epicurus, true to his beliefs, chose the secret garden over the public square.

Inspired by his founding example, the followers of Epicurus sought refuge on a metaphorical mountaintop where they aspired to lives of serenity and tranquility. From the purified heights they looked down with satisfaction (and occasional smugness) on the confused mass of humanity who lacked the wisdom to choose rightly between pleasure and pain. Their "greatest joy," Lucretius declared, was "to stand aloof in a quiet citadel, stoutly fortified by the teaching of the wise, and to gaze down from that elevation on others wandering aimlessly in a vain search for the way of life, pitting their wits one against another, disputing for preference, struggling night and day with unstinted effort to scale the pinnacles of wealth and power. O joyless hearts of men! O minds without vision!"[7]

It is not difficult to see why Epicureanism has been criticized as a socially immature model for happiness. Because it flourishes most fully in separatist groups it can become something of a cult, and by placing so much emphasis on individual self-sufficiency it can become isolating. After all, Epicureans are concerned only with how they feel. How *other* people feel does not directly concern them. True, they value justice and friendship—but only to the extent that such things affect their own lives. Whatever touches them not, concerns them not. Epicureans might care little for luxuries, but they care enormously about themselves.

PART II

Conquering Desire

3

GET BUSY WITH YOUR WORKS
(HINDUISM)

To know the secret of the universe you must drink a glass of salt water. That is the teaching of the *Chandogya Upanishad,* one of the most ancient Hindu scriptures, dating back several thousand years. (*Upanishad* translates as "sit down near," which tells us that they were originally composed as stories to be listened to, not read.) The tale is a simple one: after spending twelve years studying sacred texts with a guru, Shvetaketu returns home to his father, Uddalaka Aruni. Proudly, he declares that he knows everything that can be known. His father is a bit skeptical of this claim, but not for the reason we might suppose. We might suppose that no one could possibly know everything, even if a lifetime were spent reading books. Uddalaka Aruni, however, believed that we *could* know everything—even the innermost secret of the universe—but books were not the way to find it.[1]

Taking a more practical approach, he devises an experiment to teach his son the true nature of reality. He tells Shvetaketu to place a chunk of salt in a jug of water, leave it overnight, and then return with it the next morning. The following day Shvetaketu arrives with the jug of water. His father asks him to remove the chunk of salt. So he plunges his hand into the water and searches for it. Nothing. The salt had dissolved overnight. His father now asks Shvetaketu to sip from one side of the jug:

> "How does the water taste?" he asks.
> "Salty."
> "Now sip from the middle. How does it taste?"
> "Salty."
> "Now sip from the other side. How does it taste?"
> "Salty."

This is the secret of the universe: every drop of water tastes salty. Or, rather, this is the metaphor through which the secret is revealed. The salt water, as Uddalaka Aruni explains, symbolizes the universe—or ultimate reality, or the hidden nature of things as they truly are. Just as every drop of salt water contains salt, every part of the universe contains its own essence. Among the many parts of the universe are individual selves like you and me. So within you and me lies the essence of ultimate reality. Of course, we cannot see it, but we can trust that it is there within us—like a grain of salt dissolved in water.

Baffling though it appears from a Western perspective, the existence of absolute reality within each person is Hinduism's most fundamental truth and the basis of its teachings about happiness. As Shvetaketu's father realized, this truth cannot be acquired through mere book learning, but must be directly experienced. Hence the salt water experiment, which conveys instantly a truth that Shvetaketu never found in all the weighty tomes that he had studied so carefully. This truth, far from being distant and remote, is something we experience all the time, even if we cannot express it as philosophers or theologians. Yet we do not need to do so, for we may trust our instincts and our feelings.

Whenever we hunger for something, whenever we feel that we have not lived up to our potential, we are feeling nothing other than the presence within us of absolute reality. If we did not intuit a higher reality, then how else could we know we were not measuring up to it? As the Hindu mystic Ramakrishna (1836–1886) understood, we typically experience the absolute as a gap to be filled, a yearning to be satisfied, a bridge to be crossed: "Man is always restless, always moving from place to place.... [The] fact that he is dissatisfied with his finite nature shows that it is not his natural condition. The fact that he has infinite ambition, that he has insatiable hunger for more and more, proves that he is infinite by nature."[2]

Unsettling as Ramakrishna's words are, they are consoling, too, for we can take comfort in knowing that a feeling of discontent—the question that comes relentlessly from inside our head: *What if?*—is the blessed reminder that we are "infinite by nature." What first appear to be testaments to failure are, if we look more closely, signs of a greater reality that, at least for now, we only imperfectly understand, only clumsily grasp. The finite and dissatisfied self that we carry around day after day (like an extra suitcase we wished we had not packed) is not our true self; our true self is infinite. This means that although the universe transcends us, it also includes us.

The effort to understand such a truth is the path to happiness—or salvation, or liberation, or enlightenment, which are different names in Hinduism for the same thing. So, in this chapter, when we look at how Hindus search for enlightenment, or meditate on absolute reality, or manifest their love of a favored deity, we are looking at the multiple dimensions of the search for happiness.

But whatever form it takes, the search for happiness in the Hindu tradition begins with the intuitive knowledge that the individual and the cosmic are identical, that the essence of one's true self and the essence of absolute reality can no more be separated than could the salt from the salt water in Shvetaketu's jug. This knowledge can transform our lives by ushering in new habits of thought, action, and feeling which help us to become the greater, more developed self to which we aspire, the self that, through the power of *karma*, wins release from the eternal cycle of birth, death, and rebirth.

The *Bhagavad Gita*

Someone who struggled to become a better version of himself was Prince Arjuna, the hero of the *Bhagavad Gita* (c. 300 B.C.), the devotional poem whose popularity and authority in Hindu culture have remained unsurpassed for more than two millennia. The *Gita*, "The Lord's Song," is a poetic reflection on the duty and destiny of mankind. No aspect of human life falls outside this staggeringly audacious work.

The story opens on a battlefield, where the Kauravas are fighting their cousins, the Pandavas. (The great Hindu epic the *Mahabharata*, of which the *Gita* forms just one part, tells the full story of this conflict.) Prince Arjuna, a young Pandava warrior, refuses to fight his cousins. Krishna, his warlord companion—but actually the god Vishnu in human guise—entreats him to join the battle. Their conversation makes up almost the entire poem. After explaining to Arjuna why he should take up arms, Krishna sets out a grand view of human life, which forms the climax of the *Gita*. What appears to be a rousing battle cry becomes an awe-inspiring revelation of the universe's hidden structure and secret purpose.

Meanwhile, the rival clans, their weapons drawn, stand ready to attack each other. As a war story, the *Gita* is absurd: combat is halted while on the sidelines two soldiers contemplate the nature of the universe. But that is just the point; the absurdity of the plot tells us that plot is not integral to the story's larger meaning. The suspended battle is but the occasion, the excuse, for the main event, which is Krishna teaching Arjuna about the nature of reality.

Throughout the poem, Arjuna stands in, as it were, for us, because we, too, are searching for the key to the answer to life's great questions. (We shall come back to Arjuna soon, for he serves as a model for how we can create happiness in our lives today.) To the great and mysterious question How do we find happiness?, the *Gita* offers three answers: through the way of knowledge, the way of action, and the way of love. In truth, this is but one answer, for all three paths to happiness are manifestations of the same disciplined approach to forging a link, or closing the gap, between the self and absolute reality. This discipline goes by a name that is familiar, yet frequently misunderstood: yoga.

Yoga: Path to Happiness

An old Indian story tells of Viveka, a newborn prince, whose enemies in the royal household put him into a basket and sent it floating down the river. The infant was rescued from death by a peasant couple who raised him as their own. (This is the story of Moses, but with the social classes reversed.) Unaware of his true birth, Viveka nonetheless suspected that he had come from somewhere else, because his true mother, his true family, and his true home all appeared to him in dreams. On his sixteenth birthday he left to search for them. After journeying more than seven years, he found his way back to his true home. When he reached the royal palace, where his family had waited so long for his return, he discovered that the king, his real father, had died. Viveka knew that *he* was now king, yet struggled to find his kingly nature; raised in a world of poverty and hardship, he knew only how to be a peasant. Over time, and under the patient guidance of his teachers, Viveka cast off his comfortable yet mistaken identity and embraced the strange new reality of the person that, unbeknown to himself, he had been all along.

Of course, Viveka is not a real person, and there never was a peasant who, by some outrageous good fortune, turned out to be a prince. Viveka cannot be real because he is something more than real: he is an archetype, a revealing pattern for the course of human life. In this pattern of separation and reunion we might recognize, perhaps to our astonishment, that we ourselves feel divorced from our true nature and long to be reunited with it. Viveka's mythical search through the jungles of north India is the symbol of our actual search for our true but hidden self—hidden, yet waiting for us to find it, waiting for us to come home.

This reunion with the self, this homecoming, is achieved through yoga, the discipline that enables us to surrender our mistaken identity and recover our true one. Such a definition will appear strange to Westerners, who have experienced yoga mostly as a fitness regime of contorted and painful poses held for long stretches of time. This is a caricature, but like all caricatures, it captures a truth. Some (though not all) forms of yoga, because they emphasize posture, movement, and breath control, do indeed bring about a greater sense of physical wellbeing. Desirable such results may be, but they were not what the original yogins aimed to achieve. They sought a breakthrough in awareness, a heightened concentration of the mind—making it "one-pointed"— on the nature of absolute, ultimate reality. Long before Freud and Jung invented modern psychoanalysis, the yogins of ancient India had begun to master the unconscious, controlling its wayward impulses and irrational desires. To reach that state of unified consciousness, the yogin probably will rely on meditation and controlled breathing, but those techniques for disciplining and controlling the body are employed for the sake of the mind: to free it from distraction and desire.

Westerners who practice yoga as a form of exercise and relaxation do not always have this greater goal in mind. To understand this deeper meaning of yoga, a bit of etymology may help. *Yoga* derives from the Sanskrit root *yuj,* meaning "to link," "to yoke," or "to unite." Just what are the things to be linked? Nothing other than the individual self and absolute reality. Through yoga, the self awakens to its true identity, an identity that it discovers to be the same as the cosmos. (This is the same principle as the indivisibility of the salt and the salt water.) As one contemporary teacher has put it, yoga is a "reunion" with the truth.

Although traditionally associated with Hinduism and Buddhism, yoga remains open to those of any faith or none. It invokes no particular deity, no formal set of religious beliefs. Neither Eastern nor Western, sacred nor profane, the path of yoga is universally human. Nor is there just one path. Over the centuries, different styles of yoga have developed in India, and among the most prominent are:

- The way of knowledge (*jnana yoga*)
- The way of duty (*karma yoga*)
- The way of love (*bhakti yoga*)

We can make sense of these different paths in two ways: locally and globally. In terms of India's unique caste structure, jnana yoga developed for the intellectual elite, karma yoga for high-caste Brahmans, and bhakti yoga, the populist style, for everybody else. For our purposes, though, the global dimension is what really matters. We are interested, primarily, in what the Hindu tradition (or *any* tradition) has to say about our own search for happiness. What can we learn about happiness from this ancient culture that we cannot learn somewhere else?

The first thing we learn is that the ingredients of happiness—knowledge, duty, and loving devotion—contrast sharply with the belief so prevalent in the modern West that happiness lies in the satisfaction of physical and material desires. Duty and happiness seem to be a flat contradiction. We might avoid doing our duty (because it is unpleasant or tiresome), but never would we avoid being happy (because it is joyful and carefree, or at least that's the prevailing stereotype). But that is not how to look at things, at least not from the Hindu perspective. In that tradition, the practice of yoga tells us that happiness is not a condition of self-satisfaction, but a dynamic directed *outward,* toward knowledge of something greater than yourself, duty to your community, and loving devotion shown to others. Yoga does indeed begin with the self (where else would it begin?), but its ultimate purpose is to transcend the self by connecting it to a more profound awareness of what is absolutely and eternally real.

Second, and perhaps more important, we learn that our path to happiness must be *our* path; it must be tailor-made, suited to our temperaments and talents. There is no point embarking on the journey to happiness only to realize that you are taking the wrong (that is, somebody else's) route. Pressing the point, we could say that the three yogic paths align themselves, broadly speaking, with three different social roles or personality types: the secluded intellectual (jnana yoga), the dutiful worker and citizen (karma yoga), and the lover (bhakti yoga). To be sure, these paths are not separate and distinct—we all think, work, and love—but actually weave themselves around each other, like strands in a rope that gain strength when pulled together.

What seems to me the highest value of all these paths is that they are inclusive: *everybody,* no matter who they are, what they are like, or what they do, can find happiness in a way that is right for them. What they reveal is that our path to happiness must begin on our doorstep, where we live; otherwise it is not ours. We do not have to forge a new life—the one we have now will do just fine—nor must we wait for a more opportune moment: the right moment is always right now. To be happy we must rub *with* the grain of our character, not against it; we must become the perfected version of the person we already are, not someone we could never be. Only then can we, like the wandering Viveka, find our way back home.

The Cloud of Ignorance

Suppose you mistake a coiled rope on the floor for a snake. What you perceive through your senses, a rope, is true (you are not hallucinating), but what you make of it, a snake, is false. Deluded about the actual nature of what lies before you, you impose a wrong perception on it. But there is more. So powerful is your delusion that it begins to influence your actions. Believing the rope to be a snake, you might run away from it, try to kill it, or just stand frozen and start screaming. This illusory snake produces real effects. (If you doubt that illusions produce real effects, try explaining to the police as they really handcuff you that you were only pretending to rob the bank with your toy gun.)

To run away from a coiled rope because you believe it to be a snake is what it means to be trapped in a world of delusion: actions never fit the true state of affairs. Delusion is to be avoided for many reasons, but chiefly because it prevents us from being happy. And it was precisely to lift the cloud of ignorance, to dispel illusions, and to foster true knowledge that jnana yoga emerged in India more than a thousand years ago.

The philosopher Shankara (A.D. 788–820), the first great teacher of jnana yoga, asserted that happiness could be achieved through knowledge alone. (He meant this partly as Hinduism's challenge to Buddhism, then an upstart rival, which maintained that the secret of happiness was not perfect knowledge, but controlled desire.) The knowledge that Shankara had in mind was not anything that could be learned from sense perception (grass is green) or demonstrated through reason (all points on a circle are equidistant from the center). Rather, he meant the most profound, most intimate knowledge that anyone could possess: the knowledge that the individual self and absolute reality are identical.

Even in Shankara's day, and that was twelve hundred years ago, there was nothing new about this claim; in fact, it had been taught for centuries in the *Upanishads* (especially in the tale of Shvetaketu and the salt water). Shankara's innovation was to declare that knowledge alone was sufficient to make anyone happy. In other words, once you possess the highest knowledge you will become happy, and unless you possess it you will never be happy. Devotional acts, religious icons, and other ritualized forms of worship might inspire the necessary knowledge but could never substitute for it.

Unfortunately, this sort of knowledge is difficult to comprehend beyond a merely superficial level, as the gurus would admit. Worse, we prevent ourselves from acquiring it by stubbornly clinging to an illusion of the self. We keep on believing that the self (what makes you *you* and me *me*) is no more than some dominant aspect, personal attribute, or character trait. In ordinary conversation we often speak of people (including ourselves) as if their essence, their true nature, were confined to one obvious way in which we encounter them. We say things like "He's all heart" or "She lives in her head." Even as we give license to such caricatures we know they mislead. We all have felt the frustration not just of being misunderstood, but of being unable to put across the person that we feel we really are. Thwarted, we lament, "I wasn't myself tonight" or "She doesn't see what's inside me." Far too often, we have the lingering and disquieting sense that the person we really are, deep down, never comes into view.

What *is* this buried self that we struggle to bring to the surface? To put the question that way is to get it wrong. Wrong because your true self cannot be reduced to what someone else can experience of you, whether your body, your feelings, your thoughts, your actions, or all of them put together. Such things are mere appearances, and in time will perish. Your real self, authentic and imperishable, is the soul. Even if we learn that much from the Hindu scriptures—and it is a great deal to learn—we are still apt to mistake the soul for the *I* that we experience in normal, everyday life. The *I* that is born, grows old, dies, and is reborn (again and again, in the karmic cycle) is a false illusory self, like the coiled rope mistaken for a snake. Our true self is immortal and infinite. Until we can *experience* that absolute truth (which is something quite different from getting our heads around it) we can never find happiness, for happiness is nothing other than entering into that truth.

The story of Viveka, the peasant who discovers that he is a prince, dramatizes this very encounter with the true self. All the time there has been an absolute reality that is close to you (as close to you as you are to yourself) and waiting for you to grasp it. And when you do grasp it, you *become* the truth. When the peasant learns that he is a prince, he *becomes* a prince. Viveka does not reply, "Oh, how nice," and go back to tilling the soil. No, he quits his plough, puts on silk robes, moves into the palace, and then rules over his people. That is what it means to be a prince. And that is what Shankara meant when he taught that knowledge alone will make you happy. When you know your true self, you do not simply file away that knowledge in your mind; you feel it inside you; you live it out, just as Viveka lived out the knowledge of his royal birth. This is the core of jnana yoga: the discovery that wisdom flows effortlessly into action, like a river pouring itself into the sea.

Traditionally, the jnana yogins renounce society and give up their family, home, property, and career. Because they have learned to discriminate between the world of false appearances and the world of absolute reality, they gladly forsake the world of appearances. For who would choose to live in ignorance and delusion when knowledge and clarity are possible? (To offer a pedestrian analogy, this must feel something like the connoisseur whose refined palate makes the house red undrinkable.) The busy life of the householder—providing for a family, punching the time clock, being a good neighbor—distracts them from the contemplation of eternal truth, which has become their heart's desire.

The wisest seek refuge in a separate realm where other people's ignorance—*our* ignorance, for most of us are busy householders—will not stain the purity of their wisdom. (This is not as far-fetched as it seems, for in the medieval Christian West, monasteries and universities were created for much the same purpose, although that purpose has now all but disappeared.) We must imagine the recluse to be happy—happier, in fact, than those of us still imprisoned by our delusions as we run the race of life. He is happy because he has exchanged a world of illusion for one of perfect and pure reality.

And yet something in us refuses to pay the price of seclusion for our happiness. This is too cold, too lonely a view of life, and one that does not serve the demands of the modern world. We insist that happiness must involve others, that it *means* a certain kind of relationship with others. In defense of that view we would be quick to point out that the way of knowledge is the least trodden path to happiness. Unarguably, few among us are willing (able?) to go to such extremes to find happiness. We are not all jnana yogins, nor do we wish to be.

But that is our problem, and it reveals more about us—our weaknesses, our fears, or perhaps just the circumstances that press upon us from all sides—than it does about happiness. For the jnana yogin there is no problem at all. His exceptional life does not feel exceptional because it is the fitting response to the insight he has gained. We cannot grasp such profound wisdom and expect that our life will remain unchanged, for it is the nature of wisdom to change us. Why else do we seek it?

Take Up Your Arrows

In 1962 Indian astrologers calculated that the sun, the moon, the earth, and five other planets were about to form an ominous conjunction. So ominous that it might herald the end of the world. Something had to be done, and quickly. It fell to the Brahmans, as guardians of Hindu religious ritual, to organize elaborate prayer services, with millions of holy mantras recited across the country for several weeks. At the predicted moment, the stars and planets moved into the fateful conjunction. And then . . . nothing happened.

The scientific explanation is that astrology is nonsense, and so there never was any threat of global annihilation. Perhaps. Who knows? The spiritual explanation, and the more appealing one, is that the ritual actions organized by the Brahmans produced enough good karma to ward off the impending disaster. If nothing had been done, the planet *would* have been destroyed. The lesson is that we save the world through work, and in so doing, we save ourselves. Such is karma yoga, the way of duty. For Westerners, it is probably the preferred path to happiness, the one that suits the temper of our time and the shape and custom of our days.

More than any other Hindu scripture, the *Bhagavad Gita* takes up the theme of duty and expresses it as a problem: How, in any circumstance, do we know what action to take? It is fitting that the *Gita* opens with a moment of *inaction*: Prince Arjuna does not know whether to join the battle against his cousins. Both options are equally abhorrent: fighting means slaughtering his own kinsmen; not fighting means renouncing the sacred duty of his caste. It must have been with great trepidation, then, that Arjuna set his bow and arrow on the ground and declared that he would not fight. And yet at the same time, he sought the advice of his friend Krishna. Was he really doing the right thing? he asked. In Arjuna we are meant to see something of ourselves, and that is easy enough. Countless times in life we hesitate on the brink of action, unsure of our next step, uncertain of the way forward. So when Krishna goes on to teach Arjuna about the relationship between action and happiness, the lesson is meant for us, too.

Krishna tells Arjuna that he should do his duty and fight the enemy, even though he and the enemy are of the same blood. Arjuna need not fear the treachery of killing his own cousins because the true self—the soul—is immortal, and thus indestructible. Though the body perishes at death, the soul lives on, and in accordance with the cyclical law of karma, it passes into a new body.

But that is a dry, metaphysical proposition and not one likely to warm anyone's heart. So Krishna decides to hit home, and he tells Arjuna that it would be shameful and unmanly to renounce his obligation to fight, to retreat when others bravely advance. To preserve the well-being of his society, Arjuna must uphold the duties of his caste; if he fails, the consequence will be his own misery: "If you will not wage this war prescribed by your duty, then, by casting off both duty and honour, you will bring evil on yourself. . . . What could cause you greater pain than this? . . . Stand up, then . . . resolute for the fight."[3]

This line of reasoning persuades Arjuna to pick up his weapons and enter the fray. At last, he is ready for action. But one thing still bothers him: What *attitude* should he have toward his actions? What psychological disposition, to put Arjuna's concern into modern idiom, should he carry onto the battlefield?

Krishna teaches that we *must* act (passivity is never an option) but always with indifference, neither pinning our hopes on one outcome nor desperately seeking to avoid another. Let us be clear: we are not expected, suddenly, to relinquish all desire and motivation for action. It is not desire itself that is harmful; after all, the desire to be a good parent, spouse, or friend is still a desire. Rather, we must prevent ourselves from becoming obsessed with the *results* of what happens when we act on our desires. Our goal, then, is detachment from the fruits of our labor, whether gain or loss, joy or sorrow, praise or blame. Holding these worldly concerns at a distance, we shall come to regard them all equally. (Around the time that the *Gita* was composed, the first Stoic philosophers in ancient Greece were thinking much the same thing.)

In truth, we must look on ourselves not as the author of our actions, but as the compliant instrument through which they are accomplished. That is one of the *Gita*'s fundamental teachings. Detachment is neither passivity nor resignation, but perfect freedom—the freedom to act in whatever way seems best, seems right, for the situation at hand, because we are no longer fixated on the results of our actions. Every day we experience this freedom in small but meaningful ways. When the woman in front of you on the street drops her glove, you reach down to pick it up and return it to her. You do not stop to deliberate over your motive or calculate your chances for a reward. Thinking only of the matter at hand, you do the right thing *because* it is right. In that act of courtesy lies perfect freedom.

Such freedom can be fully gained only through discipline, which is the rousing imperative of karma yoga. Action without yoga—without control—is idle movement, just spinning your wheels or revving your engine. To give action its ultimate meaning and purpose, we must temper it through the discipline of yoga. "Stand fast in Yoga," Krishna commands. "In success and failure be the same and then get busy with your works." If you are waiting for a marching order for happiness, this is it.

In the modern world, the greatest example of a karma yogin is Mahatma Gandhi (1869–1948), whose life nobly exemplified the path of selfless service. As the whole world knows, Gandhi devoted his life to social change through nonviolence. Like Arjuna, he performed his duty in a spirit of detachment. But for all his spiritual depth, he was no hermit. In a crusading life, he battled discrimination (including the long-standing Hindu prejudice against the Untouchables), fought for the end of British colonial rule, and, after India gained independence, sought a peaceful resolution to the disputes between the country's

Hindu and Muslim populations. Less well-known, certainly among non-Hindus, is that Gandhi's favorite book was the *Bhagavad Gita* (which he first read in an *English* translation by Sir Edwin Arnold). And yet we can hardly be surprised that someone so passionately committed to action in the world regarded the *Gita,* a gospel of action, as the text that more than any other transformed his life.

It transformed his death, too. Gandhi was assassinated by a fellow Hindu who believed that he had taken the side of Muslims in the violent controversy that erupted over India's birth as an independent secular state. From that man's perspective, Gandhi had betrayed his people, but from the perspective of karma yoga, Gandhi had fulfilled his duty exceptionally well. Transcending factions and sectarian concerns, he sought the good of all humanity. He lived and died the truth that peace and harmony should prevail among all people because all of us are united in the essential oneness of being. Through his heroic actions, and for the world to see, Gandhi embodied the abstract principle that the differences between people, however seemingly indomitable, are mere illusions, and that to hurt another is to hurt yourself. That a Hindu should have murdered Gandhi is the sadly ironic testament that he had truly become detached from the consequences of action and had achieved the happiness to which that detachment unerringly leads.

But not all examples can be or should be quite so staggering. It is not difficult to see why in Indian society the inherent practicality of karma yoga—"Get busy with your works"—appeals to the vast number of people, some extraordinary, but most not, who hold down jobs, teach their children, honor their parents, comfort their friends, and serve their communities. Although the householder works, ultimately, for the benefit of all humanity (as when the Brahmans enacted rituals to ward off the destruction of the planet), he or she recognizes that even a small, seemingly insignificant action can be a form of service well rendered. *Any* worthwhile activity, however ordinary—but done in the right spirit—takes us one step closer to happiness. And because action confronts us at every moment and at every turn, the chance to be happy is always and everywhere close at hand, found in the steadiness of heart we bring to every new day, with all its looming crises and surprising adventures.

This is an encouraging lesson, and one widely applicable, as so many of us, Hindu or not, would consider ourselves ordinary householders. And it is no self-disparagement to say that, by and large, we are ordinary. Indeed, it is a good thing, for life would be unmanageable if we were all extraordinary. So if we are searching for a general truth about happiness, the Hindu scriptures tell us this: that we can find happiness in the life we already have.

Elephants Drinking Milk

Within the rich panoply of Hindu gods, Ganesha is one of the most beloved. His mother, the goddess Pavarti, created him to guard her while she bathed. One day, her husband, the god Shiva, attempted to intrude into her private chamber. Obedient to his mother's wishes, Ganesha barred his way. Shiva, furious at being prevented from seeing Pavarti—and unaware that Ganesha was his own son—cut off the boy's head. Remorseful upon learning the truth, the god vowed to restore his son to life by giving him the head of the first creature that passed by. Not unusually (for India, that is), this turned out to be an elephant.

Today, whether at home or in temples, many Hindus worship icons of the elephant-headed Ganesha, typically small porcelain figures, for his power to remove the obstacles we face in life. Through the transforming power of ritual, an icon becomes inhabited by the god whose form it depicts (and thus is much more than a statue, which is merely a lifeless resemblance). When a deity is manifest in an icon it must, like a favorite houseguest, be looked after and cared for; to neglect the icon would be to spurn the god that dwells within it. And so icons are offered food, water, flowers, clothing, incense, and, especially, praise and love. Ganesha's devotees often give him spoonfuls of milk. (About a decade ago, a miracle was said to have occurred when icons of Ganesha around the world suddenly began actually to drink the milk offered to them.) When devotees attend, in these and similar ways, to the needs of their particular god, they are not engaging in a form of make-believe, let alone lunacy. They are practicing bhakti yoga. They are finding happiness through love.

Of all the ways in Hindu culture to find happiness, love is the sweetest and most glorious. It is also the most agreeably human because it begins with something that exists naturally within all of us: the capacity—the need—to love and to be loved in return. Bhakti arouses and nourishes this capacity for love, enabling us to reveal unsuspected depths of feeling. In the Hindu tradition, those feelings of loving devotion are directed not toward humanity in general, not even toward another person, but toward god alone. It is helpful to remember that the word *bhakti* derives from the Sanskrit root *bhaj,* meaning "to be attached to" and "to have recourse to." Much more dynamic, more personal, than mere worship, *bhakti* means relying on a god—taking refuge in him or her—for protection, assistance, or some other benefit. Hence, *bhaktas* organize themselves into sects according to the particular god they worship, such as Vishnu, Shiva, Devi, or Ganesha.

Traditionally, the practice of bhakti yoga has centered not just on icons, but also on temples, shrines, festivals, and processions. Sometimes, however, this ancient path takes a surprisingly modern turn. A television adaptation of the *Ramayana,* one of the most famous Hindu epics, attracted an audience of nearly 100 million when it aired in India in the late 1980s. Watching the program's fifty-two episodes became, in itself, an act of loving devotion toward the god Rama. (The line between appearance and reality quickly blurred as the actors became identified with the gods they portrayed. Some spectators, going to extremes, lined up at the television studio to touch the actors' feet and secure a blessing.)[4] In the West, the most famous bhakti movement—and one that for many people is their dominant image of Hinduism—is Hare Krishna (the International Society for Krishna Consciousness, or ISKCON).

Whatever form it takes—feeding icons, watching television, touching feet, or parading with tambourines—bhakti yoga is all about direct and unembarrassed emotional encounters. In one parable, the bhakta is compared to a man who, finding himself in a mango orchard, does not cautiously examine each piece of fruit, noting its size, color, and weight, but simply plucks it from the tree and eats it.[5] Instead of appraising happiness from a distance, you need only reach out and grasp it. It is there for you to taste. This is a path to happiness that suits us just fine.

The path of loving devotion is direct, but still it proceeds by steps and stages: listening to and telling stories about the god, chanting his name, remembering and venerating him, making offerings to his image (like the spoonfuls of milk fed to Ganesha), considering yourself his slave, being his friend, and, finally, surrendering yourself to him. Self-surrender is the highest act, the supreme example of making one's entire life a gift to god. Nothing else expresses so perfectly the devotee's absolute love because it means being helpless before god, submitting to him utterly, and trusting in his protection.

The *Bhagavata Puranas*, a Hindu scripture composed more than a thousand years ago, speaks of bhakti yoga's all-consuming nature, when every physical and emotional resource is enlisted for devotion (here, to the god Vishnu):

Human ears that do not listen to the exploits of Vishnu are mere holes. A tongue that does not sing the songs of Vishnu is as bad as the tongue of a frog. . . . Hands, even those with flashy gold bracelets, that do not worship Vishnu are the hands of a corpse. Human eyes that do not see the emblems of Vishnu are of no more use than the eyes of a peacock's tail. . . . A heart that is not moved by hearing Vishnu's names is a heart of stone.[6]

This complete giving over of yourself in loving devotion—you have ears so that you may hear Vishnu, a tongue to praise him, eyes to see him, hands to worship him, and a heart to be moved by him—is the pure essence of bhakti yoga, and is what links it to other yogic practices. All the types of yoga that we are looking at teach the value of detachment from what confronts us in the here and now—the world and its incessant demands (jnana yoga), action and its consequences (karma yoga), and the self and its ego-driven obsessions (bhakti yoga)—for in detachment they find the secret of happiness.

The *Bhagavad Gita*, despite its emphasis on duty, affirms that happiness can also be attained through loving devotion. Bhakti gathers momentum throughout the *Gita*, and comes into its own near the poem's end, when Krishna bestows on Arjuna a "celestial eye" that enables him to behold Krishna in his true supernatural form as the god Vishnu. Krishna declares that only those "loyal-in-love" to him can ever witness such a vision. In return for such exclusive love, he promises happiness: an end to the karmic cycle of birth, death, and rebirth: "These [my devotees] will I lift up on high out of the ocean of recurring death . . . thenceforth in very truth in Me you will find your home."

Compassionately, Krishna allows anyone to worship him, regardless of caste or gender: "For whosoever makes Me his haven, base-born though he may be, yes, women too and artisans, and serfs, theirs it is to tread the highest way." Krishna's promise is more radical than we may suspect, for in the context of the highly stratified and traditional society for which the *Gita* was composed, it is profoundly liberating to declare that *anyone* can attain happiness.

But how, exactly? Apart from a famous verse that mentions offerings of flowers and recitation of holy texts, the *Gita* does not spell out specific ritual actions. Of course, that is not its purpose. The *Gita*'s purpose is to proclaim that *any* action will contribute to our happiness, as long as it is performed in a spirit of loving devotion. Then the chosen god will free his or her devotees from the cycle of rebirth and so release them into eternal bliss. Krishna's command—"Whatever you do . . . offer it up to Me"—is thus also an assurance: "those who commune with me in love's devotion [abide] in Me, and I in them."

Here again we see Hinduism's reassuring inclusivity. You need not search for extraordinary or unaccustomed ways to show your love because the right ways are all around you: *Whatever* you do, offer it up to Me. If your love is pure, then your beloved will be pleased, whatever you do; if your heart is in the right place, then happiness will be yours, whatever your life is like. Yet without the right disposition you will *never* find happiness, no matter how exhaustive your effort. "You may thrust your head into all the corners of the world," Swami Vivekananda taught a century ago, "you may explore the Himalayas, the Alps, and the Caucasus . . . you will not find it [bliss] anywhere until your heart is ready for receiving it."[7]

Frequently the relationship between the devotee and his or her god develops into a passionate fixation, sometimes bordering on obsession. The *Bhakti Sutras,* an ancient collection of sayings, tells us that the bhakta feels "joy in His [the deity's] presence, pain in His absence, indifference toward other objects."[8] How far away we have moved from the cool rationalism of jnana yoga and the earnest practicality of karma yoga. Happiness now arises as an overpowering, incomparable experience of joy. We have entered the realm of ecstasy, and with ecstasy comes risk. The risk is that the devotee will succumb to sentimentality, eroticism, or zealotry. Intense emotions play a vital role in bhakti yoga, but they must be the right sort of emotions; otherwise, the devotee might cross the line that separates the lover from the lunatic. As ever, the way to keep matters under control is through detachment from desire.

Bhakti yoga does not find easy expression in modern secular society. But still, there are lessons that Westerners can take away from ritual practices that they are unlikely to adopt in their own lives. The greatest lesson must be that the way of love, no less than the ways of knowledge and duty, directs us to be detached. In bhakti yoga there is no room for self-indulgent emotion because the emotions that count are not ours, but god's. For god's sake alone do we express our love, and not for any rapture that we might thereby obtain. We want strong feelings and we want to express them unashamedly, but the whole point of releasing such feelings is to let them direct us somewhere else, to give our life a focal point on the distant horizon. Love, because it is selfless, carries us beyond ourselves and into a vaster, possibly infinite reality. When that happens, our immediate concern for ourselves drops away like leaves falling off a tree. Thus, Krishna reserves his love only for "the man who hates not nor exults, who mourns not nor desires, who puts away both pleasant and unpleasant things. . . . I love the man who is the same to friend and foe, [the same] whether he be respected or despised, the same in heat and cold, in pleasure as in pain, who has put away attachment and remains unmoved by praise or blame."

These are cool words for the fiery art of love. Paradoxical though it seems, we learn once again that happiness lies in freedom from desire. But perhaps the greater paradox is that love, so often confused with, or at least wrapped up in, desire, gives you the strength to "put away attachment" and overcome your fixation with how the world sees you.

On the Street Where You Live

In the introduction, we touched on the question of whether there is anything to be gained from understanding happiness in terms of someone else's beliefs. Now we must face it head on, because for many readers (at least those reading from start to finish), this chapter is the first in which they encounter a religious tradition other than their own. Some will claim no such tradition; others will look warily on those who do. All that is to be expected and does not in itself derail the book's progress nor throw into doubt and confusion the reader's engagement with it. We all can understand (as distinct from accept) things we do not believe, or even tolerate.

The problem, if problem it be, with Hindu perspectives on happiness is that, despite being found the world over, Hinduism is still a local and ethnic religion. Although one in seven people on the planet are Hindus, nearly all of them live in India, and those who live elsewhere are almost exclusively from Indian families. Hinduism (unlike its cousin, Buddhism) has never been a missionary religion, and converts are rare. It is tied, inextricably and exclusively, to the culture and society of South Asia. Does this limit the insights that it might convey to people outside a prescribed set of born believers?

Hinduism's strong roots in Indian culture mean that it focuses on worldliness. Not that it teaches attachment to worldly goods (it does not), but that it teaches *how to live in the world*: how to do your duty, express your love, raise a family, help your neighbor, pursue wealth, and manage a career. Hinduism is less a set of doctrines and dogmas than a way of life (here, the contrast with Christianity and Islam could not be stronger). Certainly it has philosophical systems and abstract concepts, but its real richness lies in its diverse rituals, traditions, and devotional practices. Devotees of the god Krishna worship him by offering water, food, and flowers to his icon. The Hindu *pandit*, or storyteller, spends years memorizing several hundred thousand verses of sacred scriptures so that he can recite them to the faithful. People bathe in the sacred river Ganges because of its sanctifying and purifying powers. These are all examples of how good Hindus should act if they want to find happiness.

And action takes precedence over belief. That is really what distinguishes East from West. Eastern religions focus on the individual's search or quest, Western ones on the object of belief. The Hindu asks, What must I *do* to be saved?; the Christian and the Muslim and the Jew ask, What must I *believe* to be saved? Hindus emphasize behavior, social rules, and ritual because these give meaning to virtually every aspect of life. Meaning is woven into life's very fabric. Through its worldly disposition—"Get busy with your works," as Krishna commanded Arjuna—Hinduism makes common cause with people of other faiths or of none. That is how an ethnic religion speaks to a global audience and how the secret of its ancient wisdom about happiness is, in truth, an open one.

4

THE ENLIGHTENED ONE
(BUDDHISM)

Prince Siddhartha Gautama (c. 566–486 B.C.), known to history as the Buddha, was born in Kapilavatthu, near the foothills of the Himalayas, just across the border of present-day Nepal. His birth, like that of Jesus Christ, was heralded by miracles. He was conceived when his mother, Queen Maya, dreamed that a white baby elephant with a lotus flower in its trunk entered her side. Royal astrologers interpreted the dream as a sign of the child's auspicious, yet uncertain future: if he remained at court, he would become a great conquering warrior, but if he grew discontented with courtly life, he would leave and become a great spiritual leader. King Suddhodana, determined that his son would succeed him, consulted the astrologers once more: "How can I keep my child from leaving the royal palace?" They replied that the boy must be forever shielded from the sight of anything ugly or unpleasant. Luxury must be his entire world. Thus insulated from cold reality, he would never leave his fantasy world because he would never know that it was a fantasy.

At the moment the child was born, the earth trembled and the heavens sent down a shower of water to bathe him. Miraculously, he stood up, took seven steps (a lotus blossomed under his foot with each step), and declared "I have been born to achieve awakening for the good of the world; this is my last birth." Though but an infant, he had come to the end of the karmic cycle of reincarnation. In recognition of this marvel, the child was named Siddhartha Gautama, "he who has achieved his goal."

Heeding the warnings of the astrologers, Suddhodana imprisoned his newborn son in splendor. For many years the king's elaborate deception succeeded, and Siddhartha lived an idyllic life, free from the disquieting knowledge (the knowledge that everywhere confronts us in our lives) that people grow old, feel pain, and die. But one day, when the prince rode his chariot outside the palace, he saw something horrifying and strange: an old man. "Why," he asked his charioteer, "does the man look so sad?" Because old age is a burden, the servant replied. Siddhartha, realizing that he, too, shared the old man's fate, returned home in unaccustomed melancholy to contemplate the suffering of advancing years. The strange sights multiplied. On his next journey he saw a sick man. On his third journey he witnessed a corpse being carried to a cremation ground. And then Siddhartha witnessed the vision that would transform him: a religious mendicant, a poor holy man dressed in yellow robes who wandered from town to town, surviving on the charity of strangers.

In a flash of insight, Siddhartha knew that he must do the same. That night he stole out of his father's palace, vowing to find a new, more meaningful life among the religious ascetics who dwelt in the dense forests. He left the palace on horseback and stopped when he reached the bank of a river. There, in a ritual of symbolic rebirth, he unbridled his horse, shaved his head and beard, and exchanged clothes with a passing stranger. Siddhartha, on the outside as well as the inside, was a new man. It was the start of a great adventure: the "going forth."

The lesson of the story of the four sights is that we delude ourselves about the truth of life. The palace, that vast protective world, shields Siddhartha from true reality. Hiding inside it, he lives a comfortable, yet essentially artificial life. But he fails to realize its artificiality because he cannot imagine anything else. Until the chariot ride. The chariot ride is the breakthrough moment, the moment when Siddhartha shatters the barrier of delusion and for the first time sees the true nature of reality. But what he sees is unexpectedly brutal and bleak: we grow old, we suffer, we die.

We, too, are trapped by false beliefs, and do not even know that we are trapped. Such is the core teaching of Buddhism. Perhaps the most common false belief is that if we work hard enough or possess enough or boss others around enough, we can protect ourselves from the suffering, the loss, the heartache, and the thousand natural shocks that our flesh is heir to. But if we are ready for it, what lies ahead is the mental journey (our modern-day chariot ride) from delusion to insight and, finally, to wisdom. Which is another way of saying that it is a journey to happiness. Like Siddhartha, we can delay the journey only for so long. Something inside us—call it the dark night of the soul, a change of heart, or even a midlife crisis, so little does the label matter—compels us to leave the palace, climb into the chariot, and take to the open road. So might begin our own adventure of going forth.

Under the Fig Tree

Jolted out of complacency, Siddhartha spent the next six years in a quest for spiritual knowledge that he called "The Great Renunciation." There was nothing exceptional about his quest, for we must imagine the forests of northern India populated by monks in yellow robes, all of them begging for food, seeking wisdom, and blazing a spiritual trail. At first, Siddhartha practiced meditation, mysticism, fasting, and other ascetic rituals. But it was to no avail, and he came to realize that the path to enlightenment was the proverbial "middle way" and not the dangerous avenues of extravagance and deprivation that lay on either side. Judiciously, we must steer a course between too much and not enough. Years later, he likened the middle way to a perfectly tuned lute whose strings were neither too tight nor too loose.

Siddhartha embarked upon the middle path by staying still: he sat under a huge fig tree and began to meditate. In his honor, the tree came to be known as the Bodhi tree, or Tree of Awakening. For it was underneath that tree, on a night when the full moon shone in the month of Vaisakha, that Siddhartha woke up to the truth of all things. By sunrise he understood that for him the karmic cycle had come to its end, just as he had prophesied thirty-five years earlier on the day he was born. Having forever expelled desire and ignorance from his life, he was released into the eternal happiness known as *nirvana*. In that transforming moment, Prince Siddhartha, like a flame that is blown out, ceased to be. There was only the Buddha, the enlightened one.

Out of compassion for the suffering of all humanity, the Buddha (for so he must now be called) dedicated the rest of his life to sharing his teaching, the *dharma*, with the world. Knowing that his mission was too large to undertake by himself, he traveled to a deer park outside Benares where he rejoined five of his fellow religious mendicants. There, in the company of his earliest followers, Buddha declared himself a *tathagata*, "one who has arrived at what is so," and preached the sermon (*sutra*) that first revealed to the world the Four Noble Truths and the Eightfold Path. As the five disciples listened, they, too, gained enlightenment and were ordained the first Buddhist monks. The mission was under way.

For the remaining forty-five years of his life, Buddha preached to a growing number of followers in the surrounding villages and towns of northern India. It was during his own lifetime that monasteries were established, often by local kings or rich merchants, to provide shelter for the Buddha and his disciples when monsoons prevented them from traveling. And so the custom developed that during the summer rainy season, the monks remained together for a spiritual retreat. The monastery served not just as a welcome refuge, but also, and more important, as a living model for enlightenment, a beacon shining in a dark world. As a place where monks and nuns live and work alongside the laity, it beautifully symbolized the middle way: neither totally absorbed within society, nor completely severed from it. Even today, thousands of years later, life in a Buddhist monastery remains a rare and precious image of what the world would be like if everyone attained spiritual fulfillment.

In his eightieth year, the Buddha died peacefully in a grove of trees just outside the small and obscure town of Kusinara. Sensing that his life's journey had come to its end, he calmly prepared himself to cross over to death's far shore. He lay on his right side between two sala trees (the same tree found in the grove where he was born), with his head pointing north and one foot resting on the other. Miraculously, the sala trees bloomed out of season and showered their petals upon him. It was a sign, Buddha said, that the gods had come to be with him for his final moment of glory. Turning to the five hundred monks who assembled to witness his death, he spoke his last words: "All things of the world are passing. Strive with a clear mind to reach nirvana." Slipping into a meditative trance, the Buddha passed through to that perfect nirvana which is the extinction of identity, and its perfection. As he was released from mortal life, the gods smiled, the monks wept, the earth trembled, and thunder rolled across the open sky.

The Four Noble Truths

On the moonlit night in spring that he reached enlightenment, the Buddha found release from suffering because he had ended the seemingly endless karmic cycle of birth, death, and rebirth. His example teaches us that we, too, can free ourselves from suffering in this life—although the task is far from easy and may take many lives before we complete it. What Buddha taught about suffering—and the overcoming of it—has been long known as the Four Noble Truths:

> The Truth of Suffering
> The Truth of Arising
> The Truth of Cessation
> The Truth of the Path

These sweetly reasonable truths disclose the reality of suffering, its cause, its cure, and the path that leads to the cure. Like a doctor whose patient is all humanity, Buddha diagnoses our common illness (we suffer), determines its root cause (our desires), finds the radical cure (our suffering can end), and then prescribes it (the path that leads to the end of our suffering). These truths are noble because they enhance spiritual development and help us progress toward the happiness that is nirvana. They are noble in purpose. Yet beyond that, it takes a nobility of character to let yourself focus on suffering in the world and not be distracted by desire's siren song.

The Truth of Suffering

To put Buddhism's central truth in one sentence: Life is suffering. That is what Prince Siddhartha learned on his chariot ride when he saw an old man, a sick man, a poor man, and a dead man. To live is to become an expert in suffering, a connoisseur of suffering, as we are plagued by torments large and small of both body and mind. The most apparent forms of our suffering are pain, infirmity, disease, and, ultimately, death. Less visibly, though perhaps more damagingly, we suffer feelings of grief, frustration, and despair; we suffer negative mental states, such as greed, hatred, and addiction; we suffer, even in times of seeming contentment, boredom and anxiety. Our family is infuriating. Our friends let us down. Our pastimes are no longer pleasurable. At the worst of times we face darkness everywhere we turn.

In countless ways suffering infects the totality of life. We feel that suffering cheats us of life, steals life away from us, and puts in its place something pale and cold and lonely. So much is it a part of life that suffering accompanies even joyful events. The birth of a child—surely an occasion to celebrate—turns out to be yet another type of suffering because it places the innocent newborn in a world of disappointment and pain. We are born astride a grave, as Samuel Beckett wrote in his famously despairing play *Waiting for Godot*. Every instant of life moves you closer to death, and neither hard work nor good fortune will save you (or me) from that inevitable fate. The truth of suffering is the profoundly unsettling awareness that discontent—no, more than that: loss—is your constant companion, your intimate partner, in the journey toward your last day on earth.

How, you might well ask, can such a dark and despairing vision have anything to do with happiness? I have asked myself the same. Yet to put it that way is to ask the wrong question (one that "does not fit the case," as Buddha would say) because the question itself presumes that the truth of suffering is pessimistic, when in fact it is no such thing. The truth is what it is, and to see things as they really are is the first step toward happiness. Buddhism does not urge you to be optimistic about life or dissuade you from being pessimistic, for those are false choices. Rather, it invites you to be realistic, which is the only honest response. A truly pessimistic response would be to run away from suffering, to deny its existence. But a more helpful, and classically Buddhist, approach is to accept the truth of suffering in a heartfelt way. Like Siddhartha in his chariot, you must allow the truth of suffering, sober and cheerless though it is, not to harden but to soften you. Yes, there is suffering in the world—now do something about it. For unless you (and I and all the rest of us) show compassion for the plight of others, we have no hope of winning any happiness for ourselves.

The Truth of Arising

The law of karma tells us that everything has a cause. Buddha called this the principle of *dependent arising*: everything that arises in the world is the consequence of, and thus dependent on, something that preceded it. Suffering arises in the world, and its cause is desire. Desire is what causes us to be reborn in this world of suffering, and only when we stand apart from our desires can we, finally, escape suffering.

Some desires are sharply focused: we seek whatever is gratifying to taste, to touch, or to see. Strawberries and cream. Silk against the skin. Scarlett Johansson. Other desires, more dangerous because harder to control, feel more like inner compulsions. Buddha described this as an excessive attachment to life. He meant an insatiable drive to experience new things, to race through life with your foot pressing on the accelerator. Most of all, he meant a desire to become someone other (not someone better, which is entirely different) than the person you are right now.

In Western culture, a vivid image for headstrong desire is Faust, the man who sold his immortal soul to the devil in exchange for twenty-four years of unmatched knowledge and power. Faust desired to live more intensely than anyone in history, and having fulfilled that desire, he paid for it with the price of eternal damnation. Like all tragic figures, he realized his error only when it was too late to make amends. Although Buddha would not have accepted the story's Christian framework, he would nonetheless have endorsed its lesson: that the desire—if we indulge it—to take more from life than is our proper share, our allotted portion, will bring us only to grief.

The Truth of Cessation

But we are not doomed to bear our burdens forever. There is a cure for suffering, and the cure is freedom from our desires. The *Dhammapada*, a collection of Buddhist scriptures from the third century B.C., teaches that "whoever in this world overcomes his selfish cravings, his sorrows fall away from him, like drops of water from a lotus flower."[1] This is the Truth of Cessation: our suffering ceases when our desires are overcome.

Buddhism invites us to meditate on suffering not to be demoralized about it, not to be consumed by it, but to be released from it. Far from being mysterious, the cure for our suffering is plainly rational: to end suffering we must remove its cause, which is desire. While the logic of the thing may be easily grasped, the doing of it is not nearly so simple. But it is crucial to understand what we are being called to do. To seek enlightenment does not mean that we seek (as an Epicurean would) to remove the physical pain and stressful moments of normal, everyday life. How could we? That would be to deny life its due—even the Buddha died in pain. What enlightenment *does* remove is the mental and emotional anguish that too often threatens to take control of our life, to take possession of it, like a thief in the empty house that is us. The liberation that we seek lies in altering not life itself (that would take a miracle, which is not our line of work) but our reaction and response to it.

Among Westerners, skepticism is a common reaction to the Truth of Cessation. Perhaps you are feeling skeptical right now as you read this. Most of us would accept that curbing excess is a good and useful thing, but we would hasten to point out that some desires are legitimate and so should *not* be conquered. The desires for food, clothing, and shelter are so basic that without them life is unsustainable. The desire to protect your children, something you feel as an instinct, is part of your love for them. Even the desire for enlightenment is still a desire. So how does the Truth of Cessation make sense for normal everyday life? Not just for survival, but for a life enriched by meaning and purpose? The answer hinges on the difference between deprivation and detachment.

A few years ago, a mendicant Buddhist nun living in Hertfordshire, England, Sister Kovinda, told her story to the journalist Vicki Mackenzie, who was researching a book on Buddhist converts in the West. (Mackenzie's fascinating book is called *Why Buddhism?*) Sister Kovinda spoke candidly of how she wrestled with hunger, that most animalistic desire. The rules of her order stipulate that each day the nuns must eat their main meal out of the alms bowl; instead of buying or preparing food, they must rely on whatever they receive.

Often, this strict requirement is met through food donated by lay people visiting the monastery. But on less bountiful days, the nuns must leave the monastery, walk into the village, and do a round on the streets. Sister Kovinda cannot ask for food (let alone for anything particular), nor can she accept money. She might be given a teacake, a sandwich, or nothing at all. What she eats—*whether* she eats—depends entirely on the generosity of strangers. The ritual of the begging round is not a punishment, but something that serves a socially unifying purpose: the laity earn good karma by showing charity while the monks and nuns receive alms that aid their search for nirvana.

To endure this ordeal—how else can so uncertain an experience be described?—Sister Kovinda detaches herself from her desire for food, whether a chocolate biscuit (for which she confesses a fondness) or any food at all. She sets her desires to one side. In a practiced spirit of detachment, she expects nothing yet remains grateful for whatever she does receive. If nothing comes her way, she does not let herself become anxious. Rather, she stays calm by thinking to herself, "I'll be fine if I don't eat. . . . I'm not going to die if I don't eat today."[2] If her desire is satisfied, she is content; if it is not satisfied, still she is content. That is what it means to conquer desire: treat it with indifference.

What comes across in the interview is Sister Kovinda's honesty. There is no saintly pretense that she does not feel hunger and cravings just like the rest of us. Such feelings are human, and so there is no reason to be ashamed of them. But what emerges even more forcefully is her canniness. This street-smart nun knows the best places to conduct her rounds; she can spot the people most likely to offer her something, and she knows exactly what types of food will give her enough energy to get through the day. There is nothing otherworldly about her. Just the opposite: no one could be more harnessed to the reality of her situation than Sister Kovinda, who every day witnesses acts of charity and selfishness alike. She has answered Buddhism's call to cultivate a more detached attitude toward the things she desires, both what she possesses and what she pursues.

The Truth of the Path

How, in the intimate details of everyday life, do we lift our consciousness to a level where all these noble truths are shown to be true, so that in life we can create our own happiness? We need the truths to be something more than admirable ideas; we need them to be useful in life as we live it. Buddha's answer was the Eightfold Path: a guide for adapting our behavior in everyday life so that we will move from suffering and rebirth to the cessation of suffering and, finally, to nirvana. The path encompasses the full spectrum of human excellence, which Buddha described as wisdom (knowing things), morality (acting virtuously), and meditation (developing healthy attitudes). This is the path that leads straight to happiness.

Each of the eight steps in the path tells us what our beliefs, actions, and attitudes should be, and thus they are guides to building a better life. Wisdom, for example, means (among other things) "right action": realizing the impermanence of all things. Morality means (again, among other things) "right livelihood": not having an occupation that causes harm to others or to the world. Meditation means "right effort": controlling our thoughts so that they can be used for good purposes, such as resisting temptation. Buddha did not claim to have invented the path; it was of ancient origin, and others, in distant times, had walked it before him. He claimed only to have remembered what had been long forgotten.

When Buddha encouraged his disciples to perform "right" actions and to cultivate "right" beliefs and attitudes, he was not referring to any rules or laws handed down from on high. Buddha was no Moses on Mount Sinai, carrying down to his people the sacred tables on which God himself carved the Ten Commandments. That kind of legalistic thinking would not have made sense to Buddha, who believed that actions are right not because they conform to an established rule (no such rule exists) but because they move us forward on the path to happiness. It can be difficult for Westerners to understand that, from a Buddhist perspective, to be right means not to comply with an externally imposed rule, but to live your life, in ways both large and small, with dexterity and skill.

So instead of commanding his disciples to follow the Eightfold Path, Buddha invited them to judge for themselves whether right actions made sense in their own lives, whether such actions were useful in achieving enlightenment. If they are useful, continue with them; if not, find other ones. From its earliest days down to the present, Buddhism has freely adapted itself to the changing shape and pattern of individual lives. And that is exactly what Buddha himself would have wished, for once he compared his teachings to a sheet of gold that we are free to shape into a cloak that fits us perfectly.

In a paradox typically Buddhist, the Eightfold Path is both a path and not a path. It is a path because it leads from one place to another: from suffering to happiness. But it is not a path because it lacks a strict sequence. The eight steps—understanding, resolve, speech, action, livelihood, effort, mindfulness, and meditation—are not stages to be passed through in a predetermined order. Rather, they are the basic tasks of life that, time and again, we must work through. So they are not steps, but the occasions for action in the world. Never can we put them behind us, for their challenge is always there, confronting us in life's every moment. Nor do they come upon us in a peaceful and ordered way. They rise up all at once, in a great riotous onslaught, and we tackle them as best we can.

The Flame Blown Out

At the end of the path to happiness, nirvana awaits. Stepping off the Wheel of Life, we escape, once and forever, the imprisoning cycle of birth, death, and rebirth. That sense of escape, of leaving something behind, is crucial for our understanding of nirvana. When Buddha spoke of it, he preferred to use negative images: a lack of desire, a thirst slaked, a flame that goes out. Indeed, nirvana's literal meaning is "to extinguish" or "to blow out." What all Buddhist teachings convey is that nirvana is an experience of *not*: *not* being chained to desire, *not* having attachments, and, therefore, *not* suffering. To quote from a famous Buddhist scripture, nirvana is "not a coming, not a going, nor a standing still, nor a falling, nor a rising."[3]

Instead of thinking of nirvana as entering into a new state, we should think of it as being released from an old one. What you are released into is beside the point. The point is that you are no longer where you once were. Buddhists use various images to convey this sense of release, of going beyond. One text likens nirvana to a blossoming flower rising out of muddy water. Another says that a person who attains nirvana is like a bird escaping a net. The only thing that matters is to be set free, to no longer be trapped in the net. Most commonly, nirvana is described as a fire that has gone out; to reach nirvana means to extinguish the blaze of desire that rages inside us. Thus, Buddha spoke of the "coolness" of nirvana, for it turns down desire's broiling heat.

The happiness of nirvana can be reached in this (or a future) life, but only rarely in a full or complete way. The model is Buddha himself, who achieved both nirvana-in-this-life (when he meditated under the Bodhi tree) and the perfect nirvana attained only at death (when he was released from the cycle of rebirth). Nirvana-in-this-life is an actual occurrence and one that lies within our power. It is a complete transformation of personality characterized by peace, compassion, and joy. Negative thoughts, worries, and anxieties—all the things that get us down and hold us back—are expelled from an enlightened mind. Of course, there are degrees to this ongoing process, and we who are still searching for enlightenment can attain some of nirvana's attributes. Only a fully enlightened person, however, can possess them completely.

The time scale for enlightenment is long term in the extreme, and thus uncongenial to the modern ethos of instant gratification. If you ask Buddhists whether they expect to attain nirvana in this life, they would almost certainly answer no. But they might well raise an eyebrow or let a smile sneak across their face, because the question itself betrays a confusion about the search for enlightenment, as if it were simply one of many items to be checked off on our to-do list. Most Buddhists do not believe that they hover on the brink of nirvana and will cross the final threshold any moment now. More pragmatically, they are concerned with accumulating merit—good karma—through selfless service and compassion, thereby winning a better rebirth in the next life. And with each successive life, they will move ever closer to the ultimate goal of nirvana. But when, at last, that longed-for moment occurs, it will occur in actual life. Just like Buddha under the Tree of Awakening, they will have their own moment of blissful transfiguration.

Unlike Jews, Christians, and Muslims, Buddhists do not believe in an afterlife. They believe that when people die, they are reborn. Except for the person who achieves enlightenment. So what happens to an enlightened person at death? As Buddha himself would say, that is the wrong question to ask, because "it does not tend to edification." Merely to pose the question is to court confusion. Wondering what becomes of an enlightened person at death, Buddha taught, is like wondering what becomes of a flame that is snuffed out. Nothing *becomes* of it: the flame has not gone somewhere else; it is simply no more. Just as the flame dies when starved of oxygen, the flame of our suffering dies when starved of desire. There is no *I* who attains nirvana, because nirvana means the extinction of the selfish, all-consuming *I*.

Imagine a man wounded by a poisoned arrow. Rather than simply removing the arrow, he asks, "Who shot me? Where is he from? What kind of bow did he use?" By asking these irrelevant questions, the wounded man is only making a bad situation worse: the arrow is still piercing his flesh, still releasing poison into his bloodstream. This man, says Buddha, is the man who wastes his life speculating about nirvana. Instead of advancing him along the path to enlightenment, his pointless questions block his way. So the lesson is clear: if you want to attain happiness through nirvana, then go ahead. Walk on. "Move and the Way will open to you." But stop asking questions that do not fit the case. And pluck the poisoned arrow of suffering from your side.

If You See the Buddha, Kill Him

Always a missionary religion, although never, like Christianity and Islam, a conquering one, Buddhism has spread far beyond the towns and villages of northern India where twenty-five centuries ago the Buddha himself first preached. It became the first world religion, traveling along trade routes—the fabled Silk Road to China—over mountaintops, and across seas. As it migrated, initially throughout the Indian subcontinent and then to all of Asia, from Afghanistan to Japan, Buddhism developed into a number of schools and fashioned itself according to the local customs and traditions of the various cultures that it encountered. It took a much longer time for Buddhism to reach the West. Only since the middle of the nineteenth century has this ancient religious tradition, five hundred years older than Christianity, been seriously studied outside Asia. Of more recent occurrence, beginning in the 1960s, has been conversion to Buddhism by Westerners.

In North America and Europe, Buddhism exists not as a single religious entity, but as a plurality of congregations, monasteries, temples, and study groups, which are known collectively as the *sangha,* "the community." Indo-Chinese immigrants—the hundreds of thousands who fled their homeland in the wake of the Vietnam War—founded Buddhist communities throughout the United States, especially in California. Within these communities, monastery-trained teachers began to instruct Americans in Buddhist practices and beliefs. From this early generation of converts came the first American-born Buddhist teachers and priests. Today, the total Buddhist community (both immigrants and converts) in the United States numbers several million. A similar, though less dramatic, expansion has occurred in the United Kingdom and Western Europe, where more than a million people have converted—most of whom, it should be noted, are drawn from the white liberal educated elite.

When people enter the Buddhist community, whether as monks, nuns, or lay members, they take three vows:

> I take refuge in the Buddha.
> I take refuge in the dharma.
> I take refuge in the sangha.

The Buddha, the dharma, and the sangha are the "three jewels" of Buddhism: the example, the path, and the community. The vow is not a profession of belief, but an act of finding protection, sanctuary, and peace. To "take refuge" is to immerse yourself in something greater than and beyond yourself, to be sustained and inspired by it. This absence of religious doctrine, of a creed, has meant that Buddhism's influence in the West has been more cultural than religious.

But *why* has this ancient religion from the Far East tapped into the popular imagination of the modern secular West? Perhaps that question, too, does not fit the case. Perhaps the better, more timely question is: Why is the West *now* receptive to Buddhist teachings and practices? Why, at this point in its history, is the West poised to learn from Buddhism in a way that was not possible during periods of Western imperial and religious dominion?

The answer, surely, is that Buddhism strikes a responsive chord with so many of our concerns and values today: distrust of organized religion; demand for rational, scientific explanations; feelings of alienation from others; and obsession with the cult of the individual. Westerners who accept Buddhism do so sincerely, but they do it primarily to "repair" themselves—and society at large—by subscribing to Buddhist values. People in the West regard Buddhism as a healing faith, which is starkly different from how they probably regard the Judeo-Christian heritage: as the preservation of God's revealed word. But so strong is our need for healing that sometimes we are willing to go outside our own culture to find it.

As his death drew near, Buddha considered naming someone to lead the monastic order after he had gone, but he decided that there was no need for a successor because he himself had never been a leader. He trusted that the community would take care of itself, and so it has, for more than two millennia. True to its founder's wishes, Buddhism has never recognized a central authority—a rabbi, bishop, or ayatollah—on doctrinal matters. It is not a hard-line faith; indeed, it is not a faith at all, for there is no deity to be worshipped (Buddha was a man, not a god) but only the self to be awakened. Far from demanding strict obedience, Buddhism actively encourages questioning: test it out, try it on for size, see if it works in your own life. One ninth-century Zen master told his students, "If you meet the Buddha, kill the Buddha!" to underscore the importance of remaining independent of authority figures. The Buddha himself must be the first spiritual leader in history to tell his followers not to accept his teaching just because he gave it to them.

And that is precisely what Buddha meant when he told his disciples to turn his teaching into a golden cloak fashioned for each of them uniquely. He was telling them that the journey to happiness is always an individual, inward journey: not submission to the force of authority or passionate devotion to a charismatic guru, but a patient listening to your own thoughts, feelings, hopes, and fears. Thus, Buddhism imposes few ritual or sacramental requirements and is easily adapted to different lifestyles (there are Buddhist diamond merchants, fashion photographers, and guitar players). For those of us wary of the power wielded by large religious institutions, Buddhism is reassuringly small. And small, the saying goes, is beautiful.

Western converts to Buddhism praise its intellectual vigor, its clear explanations, and its anchored rationality. Almost uncannily, Buddhism seems to have anticipated the longings of modern scientific spiritualists, those who aspire to something beyond this plane of existence, yet also demand a cogent rationale for it. Karma, the universal law of cause and effect, is the perfect solution, for it explains logically how the past, the present, and the future are interconnected. Without resorting to either mystery or superstition, Buddhism presents a seamless explanation for how the universe works and for how each of us fits into it.

Buddhism is not so much a "believing" as a "doing," less a faith to be professed than a path to be followed. With no use for taskmasters or rule makers, its only basis is experience: to hear for yourself the lion's roar of truth. Buddha remained steadfast in the belief that even his own teachings must be tested in the crucible of experience. He did not want anyone simply to take his word for it. It is precisely this emphasis on each person's unique quest for happiness that makes Buddhism so much at home in the Western cult of the individual.

Yet there is a crucial difference. Our ego may well prompt us to learn more about Buddhism—what can Buddha do for *me*?—but the more we learn, the more we realize that the ego is a trap. To engage with Buddhism (or Hinduism) in any depth is to question the very existence of the *self* that we are trying to discover. Just who is this *me* that I so desperately want to find? Buddhism's answer is unexpected and strange: there is no enduring self; there is only the self that is continually becoming, ever evolving, always striving. To use a classic Buddhist image: the self is not a pool of stagnant water but a freshly flowing stream. A stream of becoming.

In a way that transcends psychotherapy (to say nothing of popular self-help manuals), which is all about building up the self into a stable whole, Buddhist teachings dismantle the whole project of managing the self and release us from its stranglehold. Of course, it is not that the self actually disappears, but that we come to question why so much of our life is held hostage by a pointless attempt to prop up that most cherished, and most fragile, possession: self-image.

Ultimately, though, the secret of Buddhism's popularity in the West lies in its union of spiritual transcendence and activity in the world. It answers a question that has puzzled mankind for millennia: How do you believe in something beyond yourself and yet continue to live in the here and now? It is a mistake to imagine that Buddhists are disconnected from the world, kung fu masters who speak in riddles or shaven-headed monks dressed in saffron robes. Such appearances are real, but they have nothing to do with passivity; the law of karma sees to that. For the cyclical nature of karma insists that you do only those things that you are willing to do forever.

This is a dauntingly high standard to meet. Do you want to lose your temper *forever*? Wear clothes made by children in sweatshops *forever*? Pollute the environment *forever*? You cannot dodge the question by claiming that it will be all right just this once because there is no just this once—that's what karma means. If you accept the law of karma, then you cannot wreak havoc and destruction in the world. Through the Buddhist ethic of compassion you transform yourself into someone who does not exploit the world but fiercely guards it and cares lovingly for it. You take responsibility for the world, recognizing that your every action will have untold consequences down the centuries. Detached from desire, you are happy when you hold the world at a distance, so that you may see all the more clearly how to make it better.

Prisons of the Soul

Arturo, a young Mexican American, will spend the rest of his life confined to an 8 x 10 cell in Pelican Bay Prison in northern California. He has already spent more than half his twentysome years in prisons and juvenile detention centers. It was when he was jailed for life that Arturo first learned about Buddhism. His teacher was Robina Courtin, a lesbian feminist Buddhist nun who was the first person to visit him in three years. Arturo later told Sister Robina that Buddhism "penetrated my heart and slapped me in the face." In the opposition, almost comically incongruous, between the glow of good feeling and the bracing wake-up call, those two images vividly evoke the shift from inward transformation to outward action. Buddhism begins with self-discovery, but then it rouses you to action, compelling you—with the force of a slap in the face—to seek the good of all creatures.[4]

On the day he turned twenty-one, Arturo received a birthday card from a Buddhist *lama* (teacher), who reminded him that

> we think people who are outside prison are not prisoners, but actually we are. Even people who are travelling the whole world and are regarded as successful, who think they have everything— all the desire objects—actually are in prison, the prison of their inner life because their inner life is crying, so miserable and unhappy, not finding satisfaction. They are even more unhappy than people who have very little.[5]

It is tempting to imagine how those words were received by a young man serving three life sentences. Did he find them patronizing? Did they make him cynical? Compassionate? When Sister Robina visits Arturo, who rises each day at 5 a.m., and whose first words upon awakening are taken from a traditional Buddhist prayer—"May I use this day for my own benefit and the good of others"—she is convinced that she has come to see a man who is happy. Though there is much to learn from Arturo's conversion to Buddhism, we must not romanticize it, for there is nothing sweet or innocent about it. If he leaves his cell, or is given a cellmate, he will be attacked, probably killed, by prisoners who do not understand why this ex-gang member now meditates and reads Buddhist scriptures. His survival depends entirely on his isolation. Arturo may not be in a prison of the mind, but he is in a prison nonetheless—and one that he is powerless to leave.

Let me conclude this chapter with a story of failure. Robert Thurman is a man of signal accomplishment: the first Westerner to be ordained a Tibetan Buddhist monk (the Dalai Lama himself supervised his spiritual exercises), a professor of Indo-Tibetan studies at Columbia University, and father of actress Uma Thurman. As a philosophy student at Harvard, the young Thurman lost his left eye when a tire iron slipped out of his hand and penetrated his eye socket. At that moment, Thurman, like Prince Siddhartha on his chariot ride, realized his own mortality. It's hard to resist a symbolic reading of the story: the partial loss of outward vision gives rise to a more penetrating inner vision. (In mythology, the blind man—the aged Oedipus, most famously—is the one who sees reality more clearly than everyone else.) The near-fatal accident prompted Thurman to make a pilgrimage to the Middle East and Asia, and it was during this trip that he discovered Tibetan Buddhists living in exile in India. (The Communist Chinese invasion of Tibet in 1950, which ended centuries of rule by successive Dalai Lamas, resulted in a worldwide Tibetan Buddhist diaspora.) Meeting them, he felt he had come home.

Ever since, Thurman has followed the Eightfold Path. Many of those years have been spent in Manhattan, probably the place on earth least conducive to meditation and tranquility. Still, the path is there, waiting to be walked. What is most admirable about Thurman is neither his vast knowledge nor his wide-ranging expertise, nor even his passionate commitment to Buddhism. Singularly admirable is his frank admission, "Buddhism continues to fail with me. It fails with everybody because we're still egocentric pains. I'm still self-seeking, still have problems, still get unhappy sometimes, still have worries. So it continues to fail, which means that it's not at fault, but that I continue not to use it well enough."[6]

Thurman's honesty is free from all anxiety. He watches, with classic Buddhist detachment, his own failure, beholding it from a distance. He knows that he must strive more diligently to stay on course, that his success in finding happiness is not guaranteed, and that failure, inevitable though it is, must not deter him.

PART III

Transcending Reason

5

ONLY IN HEAVEN (CHRISTIANITY)

The belief in a personal god, a belief never held by the ancient Greeks or Romans, initiated a radical change in how Westerners have thought about happiness. For those who accepted it, the historical truth of the Christian God, as manifested in both revelation (the Bible) and incarnation (Jesus, the Word made flesh), became the preeminent fact of life. One of its consequences was that happiness came to be understood, and exclusively so, as an intimate relationship with God. In the immediate postclassical world, the world of the fourth and fifth centuries A.D., the locus of happiness shifted from this life to the next. Only in the afterlife, as Christians have been taught from the earliest times, can anyone enjoy true happiness. This true happiness will outshine any happiness that we could achieve here on earth, just as God outshines humans. And yet such happiness cannot be guaranteed because it is unattainable through human effort alone and requires the gift of God's grace.

The Christian idea of a transcendent happiness would have made no sense to Seneca, Marcus Aurelius, and all the other Roman Stoics, who believed in a self-wrought happiness that could be forged right here, right now, through sheer willpower. We, too, might think that the Stoics had the better argument, for like them we tend to value self-reliance and individual initiative. Yet for early church fathers like Augustine, roused into battle against pagan cults and philosophies, this was a shocking impiety—on the scale of Prometheus stealing the power of fire from the gods. Let no one, the bishop of Hippo commanded, believe that through our own unaided effort we might achieve happiness here on earth—*that* is impossible, and merely to conceive it is sinful because it makes us God's equal.

Not until the thirteenth century, at the height of its power and influence, did the medieval church allow for a (somewhat) more earthbound approach to happiness, one that acknowledged a link between the necessarily partial happiness to be obtained in this life and the ultimate felicity to be enjoyed only in heaven. The enlargement of the traditional Christian idea of happiness was the work of two men: a dead pagan philosopher from Athens and a young Dominican friar from southern Italy. The pagan was Aristotle.

The Dumb Ox

In the castle of Roccasecca, north of Naples, where he was later imprisoned by his brothers, was born the youngest son of the Conte d'Aquino. History—and heaven—knows him as Thomas Aquinas (1224–1274), saint of the Roman Catholic Church, author of the *Summa Theologiae*, and reconciler of reason and faith. The scion of an aristocratic family (his great uncle, Frederick Barbarossa, had been the Holy Roman Emperor), Aquinas was sent at age five to be educated at the Benedictine monastery at nearby Monte Cassino. His father, partly to find a useful career for his quiet, but thoughtful seventh son, and partly to make amends for having sided with the Holy Roman Emperor to sack the monastery, proposed that the young Thomas be received as a Benedictine monk. Because worldly rank mattered in a medieval monastery, and especially there, the boy was tapped as a future abbot of Monte Cassino. All problems resolved.

And then it fell apart. Aquinas went on to study at the University of Naples, where he came under the enlightened influence of the Dominicans, a new order of mendicant preachers and, at that time, among the few people in Christendom to have read the newly translated works of Aristotle. (We shall come back to Aristotle's influence, for it explains much of what Aquinas believed about happiness.) His head stuffed with radical new ideas, Aquinas promptly returned to the family castle and told his father that instead of becoming the feudal lord of a monastery he would spurn the trappings of nobility and beg for his food as a poor friar. The news did not go down well.

Family honor was at stake, and the turncoat Thomas had to be turned back again. His brothers kidnapped him and for a year held him prisoner at Roccasecca, as if he were no better than a serf who had stolen a mule. But Aquinas, not yet twenty, had a mule's stubbornness, and he refused to yield. So the brothers tempered their vengeance and tried to persuade him with earthly delights. One night, as Aquinas slept, they smuggled a beautiful young woman into his chamber in the hope that lust would get the better of him. How despicable their hope was, for they knew that he had already taken a vow of celibacy. What they failed to count on was the strength of that vow. Awaking to the erotic vision, Aquinas leaped out of bed, brandished a flaming torch, and chased the poor shrieking woman out of the room. He bolted the door behind her, and then, in a rare display of violent anger, thrust the firebrand into the door, burning into the blackened wood a sign of the cross. His brothers, shamed and defeated, set free their chaste sibling, who left immediately for Paris, where, at last, he entered the order founded by St. Dominic.

In Paris, and later Cologne, Aquinas studied with the German theologian Albertus Magnus, better known as Albert the Great. Great because he was unafraid of science and reason, especially when explained by pagan Greek philosophers or Muslim scholars. Among the religious novices who flocked to his lectures was, in G. K. Chesterton's description from his marvelous little biography, "one student, conspicuous by his tall and bulky figure, and completely failing or refusing to be conspicuous for anything else."[1] This young man was so silent in classroom debates, and so lumbering in his walk, that his schoolfellows cruelly nicknamed him the Dumb Ox. Yet Aquinas (for it was he) knew more than he let on. Albert knew the humility of genius when he saw it, even if others were blind; prophetically, he retorted, "You call him a Dumb Ox; I tell you this Dumb Ox shall bellow so loud that his bellowing will fill the world."

In 1252, Friar Thomas returned to Paris, where he finished his studies and began his teaching career. In later years he was assigned to Dominican houses in Naples, Orvieto, and Rome (as a mendicant friar, he made all these journeys on foot), where he lectured, preached, and began to write his unfinished masterpiece, the *Summa Theologiae,* "The Summation of All Theology." It was in the *Summa*—a work that for centuries has been caricatured, mostly by those who have not read it, as nothing but pedantic distinctions and pointless speculation about angels on pinheads—that Aquinas devoted so much respectful attention to mankind's pursuit of happiness.

For twenty years Aquinas kept up a driving pace of intellectual labor, writing more than forty books (dictating, actually; his handwritten scrawl was indecipherable). But in December 1273, at the Benedictine priory in Naples, where he was drafting a treatise on the sacrament of penance for the *Summa,* something extraordinary, and extraordinarily mysterious, happened to him. As he celebrated Mass on the morning of the 6th of December, the feast day of St. Nicholas, Aquinas was struck by some miraculous vision or mystic insight, the details of which he never shared, not even with his intimate friend and confessor, Friar Reginald of Piperno. From that day forward he never wrote another word, never dictated another sentence to his scribes. As if in a perpetual trance, he devoted himself entirely to prayer. Reginald, puzzled by this behavior (the friars joked that Aquinas dictated theological treatises in his sleep), implored him to return to his great unfinished work. Wearily, and impatiently, too, Thomas replied, "After what I have seen, all that I have written seems like straw to me."

Why this prodigious scholar, not yet fifty, so abruptly abandoned his life's work remains a mystery. Did he fall ill? Did he succumb to nervous exhaustion? Perhaps he suffered brain damage from a stroke; the other friars observed that he had difficulty speaking and walking and seemed constantly dazed (*stupefactus*). The miracle-seeking hagiographers who wrote the earliest biographies of Aquinas attributed the overnight change to a mystical experience in which he realized the essential futility of expressing the divine in human terms.

Whatever its cause, the sudden renunciation was an ill omen: within three months he was dead. Early in the new year, he had been called by Pope Gregory X to attend the Second Council of Lyons. At the beginning of February he and Friar Reginald headed north for France. They had been traveling only a few days when Thomas struck his head against a tree branch that hung over the road. The injury proved to be fatal, and on the morning of the 7th of March 1274, lying in the guesthouse of the Cistercian abbey at Fossanova, south of Rome, Thomas Aquinas entered history as the greatest mind that Christianity had known in nearly a thousand years.

Learning from the Pagans

When the invading armies of Alaric sacked Rome in A.D. 410, the lamp of Western civilization, if not exactly extinguished, was turned down to a flicker. Eight hundred years would pass before the works of Aristotle, the common currency of educated Greeks and Romans, resurfaced in the Christian West. For nearly a millennium, the Islamic world, stretching from India to Spain, preserved the heritage of classical antiquity. This heritage Europe reclaimed for itself alone, even though the great Muslim intellectuals Ibn Sina (Avicenna; 980–1037) and Ibn Rushd (Averroës; 1126–1198) were translating and writing commentaries on Greek and Latin texts when Europe was still imprisoned in the proverbial Dark Ages. In an irony of the time, Christian Crusaders in the Middle East were intent on demolishing Islam while Muslims in Spain were shoring up the West's intellectual foundation.

Beginning in the thirteenth century, the writings of Aristotle, and learned essays on them, appeared in southern Europe in Latin translations of Arabic versions and the original Greek texts. The Latin texts were sent to monasteries and to the handful of universities—Paris, Toulouse, Bologna, Cologne, Oxford, and Cambridge—then in their infancy. (Medieval universities were themselves religious institutions, for the pope often granted their charters and theology was one of their principal subjects.) It is sobering to remember that Aristotle was twice as remote to the Middle Ages as the Middle Ages is to us. Whereas more than seven hundred years separate us from Aquinas, fifteen hundred distanced him from the pagan philosopher. To someone in the Middle Ages, classical antiquity was a remote civilization, more remote than it seems to us today.

For medieval Christianity, the rediscovery of classical thought was not an entertaining prospect but a pernicious threat that shook the Church to its core. Suddenly, and without welcome, here was a body of knowledge, a way of understanding the world, that had been hidden for centuries. Hidden, that is, from European Christians, for whom Aristotle's treatises tackling the biggest of the big questions—ethics, politics, science, and metaphysics—came as a disturbing revelation.

They were sweeping in scope, persuasive in rationality, and untouched by Christian doctrine. At times they contradicted it, and thus gave license to the heresy that revealed biblical truth—the Word of God spoken through his prophets—was not the only truth available. To study a pagan philosopher whose ideas threatened the very basis of Christian belief was, to put it mildly, a risky business.

As risk averse as any multinational organization, the medieval Church, in the person of the archbishop of Paris, banned outright every single word that Aristotle had written. But thought crimes continued to be perpetrated, and nowhere more successfully, or more creatively, than among ecclesiastics themselves, who stole into the *scriptoria* of monasteries across Europe to read Aristotle's intellectual pornography.

Over time, however, the Church adopted a shrewdly accommodating stance, recognizing the strategic benefit of using Greek philosophy to elaborate Christian doctrine. For a rising generation of scholastics, the new challenge was not to censor Aristotle, but to refute whatever in his writings contradicted biblical revelation, to retain whatever was consistent with Church teaching, and, above all, to emulate the philosopher's rigorous analytical method. The approach sounds iniquitous, but its goal was a generous one: to prove that there was no fundamental conflict between Christian theology and Greek philosophy, nothing incompatible between faith and reason.

Known as the Great Synthesis, this heroic intellectual project was begun in Paris by Albert the Great and completed in Naples by his prize pupil, Thomas Aquinas, the bellowing dumb ox. It is a cliché among theologians (and an offense among classicists) to say that Aquinas baptized Aristotle. A less exaggerated appraisal might be that he made the Christian world safe for Aristotle's rational and pragmatic way of thinking, especially about things like happiness. For no one has been more responsible than the humble Dominican friar, undaunted as he was by judgmental traditionalists, for weaving the logical system of a heathen philosopher into the patterned, if now tattered, cloth of Christianity. Logic, when placed in the right hands, could become a very useful tool for surveying the path to happiness.

Faith and Reason

Blessed with a sunny Mediterranean outlook, Aristotle took for granted that the world originated in an eternal goodness and possessed a fundamental order and purpose. More gloomily, Christians believed that the world, although originally created by a good and loving God, was corrupted when that temptress Eve gave to Adam the forbidden fruit. Right from the start, the dilemma for Christians has been whether to emphasize God's goodness or man's wickedness.

For Aristotle, the concept of original sin would have made no sense; it was a form of self-punishment, and no rational person, he believed, would choose to punish himself. Aquinas, although not free to ignore the reality of sin, could still accentuate the positive part of the story of Genesis. By keeping the spotlight, as it were, on divine benevolence, he found a way to reflect on God's unconditional love for us and his wish that we be happy. Indeed, true happiness, as Aquinas understood it, consists in nothing other than the contemplation of God's essence. Although such perfect beatitude cannot be attained in this world, the world has been created so that, by leading a virtuous life, we may prepare ourselves for the ultimate happiness that awaits in heaven. Scarred and disfigured though our sins have made it, the world exists not for our misery, but for our joy.

Aquinas never doubted that God *wants* us to find happiness. At the moment of creation, the creator pointed us in the direction of bliss. Of course, we humans have only two ways of knowing what God wants:

faith and reason. It is no secret that many religions have their suspicions about reason, and Christianity has been no exception. As that legendary pessimist Augustine taught, reason—the ability to distinguish between true and false—is fallible and so can become the instrument of pride and deception. Biblical revelation and Church doctrine, he preached, are the sole guides to unerring truth. Aquinas took much from Augustine, but he did not take it hook, line, and sinker. He was not willing to declare that faith and reason are in conflict. Just the opposite: they are in harmony (although at times the harmony is tuned to a pitch beyond our hearing), and the lowliest fact can lead us to the highest truth.

There must have been something of the Neapolitan peasant in Aquinas, for he was commonsensical enough to believe that God gave us a mind so that we would use it and seek to know the nature and cause of all things, including himself. But reason is reasonable enough to know its limits. (Only the deluded man believes his powers are boundless.) On reason's wings, we fly high, but not so high that we touch the face of God, for the finite cannot know the infinite. As Aquinas put it, a mere "created substance" cannot know a "divine essence."[2] So our natural desire to know absolutely everything can be fully, completely, and lastingly satisfied only through revelation, which is how God unveils his identity to mankind. Yet revelation is not the adversary of reason, but its fulfillment and perfection. Reason, although necessarily limited, composes a wisdom and does not ensnare us in delusion's trap. Reason is how we enter into God's plan for our happiness, how we know what happiness means.

This way of thinking tells us why the Dark Ages is so appallingly misnamed. Though the lesson was lost in later times (and is still lost for some), the medieval Church declared that there can be no ultimate contradiction between what reason tells us and what faith gives us. Those two lamps of knowledge shine each upon the other. In our moment of globally resurgent religious fundamentalism, the thirteenth century suddenly, and to our shame, appears more modern than the twenty-first.

The Magnetic Pull of Truth

Nowhere is the perfection of reason through faith more evident than in the *Summa Theologiae,* the monumental work that Aquinas began in 1265—and then refused to finish because of his own inner or mystical experience. Incomplete though it is, the *Summa* stands as the foremost example of medieval scholastic theology, which means that its goal is not to explain this or that biblical passage but to organize the totality of revelation into a logical and systematic whole. The *Summa* is an enormous magnet that draws in the many disparate truths that God has revealed to humanity throughout history, finding unity where there seems only puzzling diversity.

For all its high intellectual ambition, Aquinas wrote the work *ad eruditionem incipientium*: for the instruction of beginners, as he states several times in the preface. A devoted teacher, Aquinas was thinking of his students and their need, not for hair-splitting scholarship but for a grand overview of the logical coherence of divinely revealed truth. He had the gift of all great teachers, which was first to immerse himself in deep learning and then to condense that learning so that it could be grasped in its totality by even the densest pupil. And yet it is precisely the astounding scope and measured pace of Aquinas's work that will frustrate modern readers, accustomed as we are to absorbing knowledge rapidly and in bits and pieces, through sound bites, slogans, and headlines. The merest glimpse of a single page from the *Summa* will reveal it to be tightly structured, dauntingly dense, and altogether lacking in warmth and charm.

Each of the *Summa*'s three long parts is divided into formally stated questions on distinctive topics, such as "Does happiness consist in earthly goods?" Each question, in turn, is subdivided into articles that examine particular issues within the stated topic, such as "Whether wealth is necessary for happiness" (wealth being one of the "earthly goods" under discussion). To answer the several queries posed in each article, Aquinas follows a fixed method: he lists, as precisely as possible, the objections to his own view; he makes his case, quoting relevant theological and philosophical texts; and, finally, he refutes each of the objections that he had so carefully stated at the outset.

The *Summa* contains 613 questions divided into 3,125 articles, with nearly 10,000 objections and refutations. Each article, which really has the character of a conversation or dialogue, begins with the interrogative *ultrum* ("whether"), that one word signaling that the matter is not settled in advance, but is that rare thing: a genuinely open question. The answers offered (and there are thousands of them) are not fixed or final but provisional and subject to future discussion and debate. Provisional not because truth is arbitrary, but because it is mysterious and many-sided. In its spirit of discovery and dialogue, the *Summa* feels surprisingly, but reassuringly, modern.

What seems alien to us, though, is its precision and formality; there is nothing casual about Aquinas's prose. But that is exactly what his original readers would have expected. In its structure, the *Summa* derives entirely from the medieval *disputatio*, the highly ritualized classroom debates conducted by eagerly adversarial religious novices. Aquinas stuck to this approach for the sensible reason that he knew it best, having mastered it while studying with Albert the Great in Paris and Cologne. We need to picture the young Aquinas participating in these academic games—hesitantly, though; he was still the dumb ox—alongside scores of other young men who, although more combative, were far less clever.

How might this remnant of a long-vanished moment speak to us today, particularly to those of us who stand apart from its untroubled presumption of religious belief? In our time of abrasive journalism and political debates that quickly descend into juvenile retorts, it is easy to miss what is (for us) most unusual about how Aquinas argued his points: that he fought not *against* his opponent but *for* the truth. That is why he began every argument by stating his opponent's view not in the weakest, but in the strongest, terms. Indeed, he starts not as the aggressive questioner but as the patient listener; with goodwill, he tries to reckon with the position of those who disagree with him. Only in that way will an argument be convincingly overthrown—not by the witty phrase or the rhetorical turn, still less by name calling and fist thumping. For Aquinas, an intellectual dispute was no jousting match, in which competitors tried to unseat one another, but a common search for truth. Truth as it could be demonstrated—to everyone—by the light and guidance of reason.

The truth about happiness, as Aquinas believed it, is found in the second part of the *Summa,* where he discusses human action. The Latin term for happiness, and the one that Aquinas uses throughout, is *beatitudo.* For Christians the word immediately calls to mind the Sermon on the Mount, when Jesus spoke the beatitudes: "Blessed are the meek," "Blessed are the poor," and so on. (We might think of that famous sermon as a public preaching on happiness, something akin to a Christian version of Buddha's sermon in the deer park at Benares.) What is contained in the word *beatitudo* is precisely this sense of "blessedness": not simply a higher or better state of being, but one that is closer to God, warmed by his radiance. This state of drawing near to God is the core of Aquinas's vision of happiness and one that today we might find confusing, irrelevant, or even offensive. But, generous interlocutor that he was, Aquinas anticipated our doubts. He tries to persuade us through reason, and reason alone, that perfect happiness exists only in heaven, in the contemplation of God's essence. Those who know their catechism will recognize this as the "beatific vision."

Happiness, the Final Frontier

Aquinas presumes that humanity is naturally curious, and thus he shares Aristotle's conviction, expressed in the opening sentence of his *Metaphysics*, that "all human beings by nature desire to know." To know, however, is not merely to gather up information, but to seek out origins and uncover causes. (Example: to know why objects of unequal weight fall at the same speed is to uncover the law of gravity.) Although it appears forward-moving and progressive, knowledge is actually, Aquinas says, a working back toward first principles. We gaze with wonderment upon the world and are moved to know who created it, and why. It was no innocent thing for Aquinas to believe that humans are naturally curious, for such a belief declares that knowledge could *never* be a forbidden fruit.

One thing that we can know is ourselves; we can seek to discover the purpose and meaning of *our* existence. As good rationalists, we begin that voyage of discovery with the guiding principle that each living thing has a distinctive purpose or state of completion toward which it naturally tends. This state of completion, which Aquinas called "specific perfection" (a concept he learned from Aristotle), varies from creature to creature according to its distinctive capabilities: seeds grow into fruit-bearing plants, caterpillars turn into butterflies, frolicking colts become tamed horses, and impetuous children mature into rational adults. By "perfection," Aquinas does not mean flawlessness but rather the complete attainment of what a thing is supposed to be. (When someone says he is perfectly satisfied, he means that he is completely so.) Humankind is unique among all living things because it enlists reason to seek its perfection. We act deliberately to move ever closer to the fulfillment of our natural purpose, thus becoming most truly ourselves.

In Aquinas's discussion of happiness, the starting point is that whenever we act, we act for a purpose: "Each thing desires its own fulfillment and therefore desires for its ultimate end a good that perfects and completes it."[3] Just as we climb a staircase to reach the top, we undertake action to achieve a certain outcome. In that sense, all human actions, provided they are guided by reason, are purposeful movements toward intended goals. (Involuntary mechanisms, such as blinking, sneezing, and growing older, are the exceptions.) Our goals are neither scattered nor isolated, but arranged in a logical hierarchy. We work to earn money; we earn money to pay our mortgage; we pay our mortgage to have a secure home; we have a secure home to provide for our family. And so on. But where does it end? Is there a last link in the chain of our goals?

Aquinas was certain that there *must* be a final goal to guide our every action and to impose coherence on the chaos of our lives. Instead of contending with an infinite series of purposes, inevitably in conflict, we need to stay focused on the supreme, governing one. Just as a train makes intermediary stops but has only one terminus, we have intermediary goals but only one final end. Whatever we do and whatever we desire, we do and desire it for the sake of this ultimate goal. If we lacked such a final purpose, we would never experience any moment of accomplishment, for there would be nothing to accomplish. It would be like shooting arrows without a target: you would never hit the bull's eye because it would not be there for you to hit.

But what *is* this target that we all aim at? What is this single point of destination toward which you and I are headed? It is nothing other than happiness. This is no mere greeting card pleasantry. For when Aquinas asserts that eternal beatitude—everlasting happiness—is the true end of human life, he does not mean anything so trivial as that happiness is a nice thing to have and we should do all we can to find it. No, his meaning is far more urgent: that happiness is your complete and perfect good; that God created you to be happy; that your desire to be happy is natural. And just as it is unnatural for a plant to hide from the sun, it is unnatural for you to hide from happiness.

Our Heart's Desire

For Aquinas, the only definition of happiness that can be logically defended is the perfect happiness that consists in the heavenly vision of God. As the supreme object of desire, God overrides, indeed obliterates all lesser desires. This, Aquinas argued, stands to reason: because we desire things in proportion to their goodness, we desire God most of all because he alone is infinite goodness. But some of us stand in reason's cold shadow, not its warming light. We are trapped by inferior versions of happiness, mistakenly believing that a "created good"— anything that exists in the world or is part of our own being—can make us truly happy.

Like so many of the world's great thinkers about the good life, whether Epicurus, the Stoics, or Buddha, Aquinas believed that no worldly possession—wealth, honor, power, or glory—can make you happy. Wealth, whether money or the things that money can buy, is always sought for the sake of something else: at the most basic level, food, clothing, and shelter. To desire one thing for the sake of another is to desire it as the means to an end, but not as the end itself. Because happiness is the *ultimate* end, it cannot be found in wealth.

Nor can we equate happiness with honor, because honor is not a character trait but the deference shown by one person to another. (As children, we honor our parents when we abide by the decisions they make on our behalf.) Honor recognizes excellence, but is not excellence itself. Still less can happiness reside in glory, for glory is nothing but public praise, and yet praise can be unmerited. (The modern word for false glory is "celebrity.") That would make happiness the product of imperfect human knowledge, and thus prone to error. Finally, happiness cannot be found in power, because although happiness is a perfect good, power can be used for evil.

It would be just as wrong to assume that happiness is an internal good, as if the perfection of the body (the whitest teeth, the firmest breasts, the silkiest hair) were somehow morally superior to the pursuit of worldly goods. As Aquinas explained, everywhere we look nature tells us that happiness does not consist in bodily perfection, whether superior strength, robust health, or exceptional longevity. A human being is happier than any animal, yet deer are faster, lions stronger, and tortoises older. Moreover, the goods of the body serve only to preserve life and do not aim at anything greater. That puts them at odds with the view of happiness as a goal, because goals imply movement toward a destination. Anyone who claims that his or her goal is self-preservation is as ludicrous as a marathon runner who thinks he can win by running in place: what matters is moving toward the finishing line.

Aquinas would tell you that although you're meant to enjoy worldly goods and goods of the body (it's all right to live in a nice house and to get a good haircut), you mustn't mistake that enjoyment for true happiness. Of course, the millionaire rejoices in his wealth, the diplomat in her reputation, the film star in fame, the runway model in beauty, the Olympian in strength, and the Nobel laureate in genius. But only a limited, and thus unsatisfying, happiness can be derived from those attributes, because they are passing, not permanent. Even if you were amazingly rich, highly esteemed, globally famous, stunningly gorgeous, fearsomely strong, and prodigiously intelligent, it would not be enough. Your happiness would be undermined by the nagging feeling, the creeping fear, that something could go wrong. The only time nothing will go wrong for you, the only time all your desires will be satisfied, Aquinas said, is when you make God himself the consummation of your desires.

Deep (and High) Thoughts

Unlike God, who is happy in his own essence, we must search for and achieve our happiness. For Aquinas, that achievement is a union with God, a sharing or participating in the divine uncreated good. Here again we glimpse the shadow of Aristotle, who also insisted that happiness was an activity: a purposeful movement toward fulfillment. By "activity," Aquinas had in mind a rather particular kind of effort. He did not mean mere motion, such as walking or running, or acting on an object, such as chopping wood. Nor did he mean a preference for worldly affairs, for living what we commonly call an "active life."

Activity is something truly dynamic: the progression from potentiality to actuality, immaturity to maturity, and imperfection to perfection. When we say that the time is ripe, or that a friend, previously shy and retiring, has suddenly blossomed, we are getting close to the *developmental* sense of activity that for Aquinas was such an important dimension of happiness. The thing to be developed most of all is life itself. Your life shouldn't just ramble along, one damn thing after another, but should move purposefully toward a final, fulfilling goal.

For Aquinas, the supreme activity of life is the search for happiness, and it is conducted through the intellect. This much stands to reason: because happiness is your highest end, its attainment must rely on your highest faculty, which is the intellect. (Though followers of St. Francis of Assisi would argue that love is your highest faculty.) But the part of the intellect that really interested Aquinas is contemplation, which he regarded as the highest function of our highest faculty. In other words, contemplation is the single greatest activity that you (and everybody else) can undertake.

To be happy we must contemplate, but we cannot contemplate just anything: a daisy, a Calvin Klein model, or the second law of thermodynamics. Because happiness is our highest end, we must use our intellect to contemplate the highest object, the most final and absolute thing that can be known. Only one entity, Aquinas believed, meets that criterion: God, the architect and governor of the universe. The happiness we derive from contemplating him will be perfect (and cannot be anything *other* than perfect) because God, the first cause of everything, is perfection itself. Only in this "vision of the divine essence," Aquinas declared, can we attain "ultimate and perfect happiness."[4]

Face to Face

Like other religions, Christianity offers a powerful rebuke to the seeming appeal of earthly fortunes and worldly goods: they fail to merit our exclusive attention because they fail to make us supremely happy. Augustine pessimistically believed that no happiness was possible in this life except for the mere hope of happiness in the next. (If you were a nervous Roman and the barbarians were at the gate, you might think the same thing.) But Aquinas inclined toward the more balanced view that in this life we can be allotted a share of the plenitude of happiness that waits in heaven. In a cheerier mood, he explained that humanity can indeed participate in celestial happiness (*participatio beatitudinis*).

Even so, Aquinas's perspective is asymmetric. Happiness in our lifetime must always fall short of perfect happiness in heaven because the divine essence (the contemplation of which *is* happiness) remains hidden to us here on earth. Agonizingly, we feel that some part of God remains inaccessible, and we suffer in our painful awareness that as long as the beatific vision is eclipsed we cannot know true happiness. God's essential nature must, for now, remain a mystery to the human mind, for "all that man knows of God is to know that he does not know him."[5]

The frustration we feel at being separated from God is no mere annoyance, like being cut off on the telephone or missing a train. It is, rather, a profound feeling of helplessness: we were made to know God (Aquinas never doubted that), and yet we cannot know him; we cannot achieve our own destiny. We search the world for God, but never do we find him. At best, we see only his trace, his fingerprint. The miracle of birth is a sign that God created us; the laws of nature reveal his genius; the thunder roars his potency; and the distant stars shine with his infinity. As the poet Gerard Manley Hopkins rhapsodized, "The world is charged with the grandeur of God." But the world is not charged with God himself. Of him we know nothing—and yet on him our happiness depends entirely.

So we are left with the unsettling, and yet optimistic, belief that to be happy, completely and everlastingly happy, we must behold the divine essence that is nowhere found on earth. The New Testament writers assure us that what we will find in heaven is no mere reflection or image of God (such as we encounter in the world) but an actual vision of his pure being. As St. Paul famously told the Christians of Corinth, "For now we see through a glass, darkly; but then face to face." What the Damascene convert meant was that, once apprehended, the beatific vision gives us clear, immediate, and direct knowledge of God, far beyond the shadowy knowledge available to us here on earth, where we must approach divinity indirectly, through symbols, signs, and allegories. The brilliance of the vision will never fade, Aquinas contended, for "the mind of man will be united to God in one, continual, everlasting activity."[6]

Amazingly, Grace

Striving, in this life, through reason and virtue, we can attain only a hint of the complete and everlasting beatitude that awaits us in the hereafter. Incapable as we are of becoming perfectly happy "through our own resources," we rely on God's help.[7] As we stand on the threshold of celestial bliss, unable to cross over, God comes to our rescue. He raises us up through the gift of his grace.

Like all gifts, grace is unmerited. Aquinas was perfectly clear about that. God freely gives his grace to a sinful, undeserving humanity, a humanity that can never earn such a bounty, but only accept it. We desire to know God because God himself instilled the desire in our hearts from the first moment of creation. God made us to be reunited with him, and it would be a perverse God who denied his creation the possibility of satisfying that most natural of desires.

But the gift of grace does not absolve us of responsibility, as if we could just lie around waiting for grace to drop out of the sky and shower itself upon us. No, we must meet grace halfway, Aquinas insisted. We must do our bit, make our own effort to be virtuous. For virtue, the foundation of imperfect, earthly happiness, will orient us toward perfect, celestial happiness. Virtue will point us in the right direction. Here, what Aquinas had in mind are the traditional Aristotelian moral virtues of justice, courage, temperance, and prudence, along with the classically Christian virtues (Aquinas called them "theological virtues" because they flow from God) of faith, hope, and charity. They are the habit, or disposition, to do the right thing. Through God's grace we take our final step on the path to eternal happiness, but just to put ourselves on that path we must act virtuously. In the pursuit of happiness, virtue is the minimum requirement. We are gravely mistaken if we believe that in this life we can commit acts of malice and atrocity and then suddenly, through divine grace, find ourselves transported into the realm of eternal bliss.

The Thundering Silence of
St. Thomas

The exquisite irony of the life of Thomas Aquinas is that the last message of this man so driven to express himself in the steady drumbeat of words was . . . silence. Silent not because he had nothing more to say, but because there was no way of saying it. Aquinas had reached down to the deep inexpressible mystery of things and touched on a truth that words fail utterly to convey. This silence, which not even his devoted sister could break, nor his dearest companion, Friar Reginald, lasted to the moment of his death.

The great *Summa* was left unfinished not because death stayed the author's hand, but because the author had lived long enough—no, profoundly enough—to realize that the works of the hand can never express the wonders of the heart. Like other theologians of his time, Aquinas had learned about a wise Persian mystic from an earlier century named "Algazal." Perhaps when his own mystical vision descended upon him, the Christian monk gained a deeper appreciation for the Islamic scholar's conviction that silence, just as much as words, can express the truth.

What the vision must have brought home to Aquinas was that the true essence of things is unfathomable, and in the last resort reason cannot find it. No answers we can give will ever be sufficient for the questions we want to ask. And yet there is a way to know the things that the mind cannot grasp. This way has nothing to do with reason and logic, but everything to do with the transcending of it. Our response to the limitations of reason, to the boundaries of our own minds, cannot be to forsake reason, for that would be only to drown in the deep swirl of ignorance. What is required is something *other* than reason. For want of a better word, we may call it imagination, although it has been called other things over the centuries: mystic ecstasy, meditation, or simply prayer. Of course, we need reason to lead us to imagination, just as we need a boat to travel across the water. But once we have reached the shore, we must get out of the boat to travel further inland. In the same way, reason will have served its purpose when it is used up, and we have no choice but to leap beyond it.

Aquinas made just this sort of transcendent leap, or rather it came upon him in the vision that struck him dumb while he celebrated Mass on a cold December morning in 1273. We are drawn back to the story of the final days of Thomas Aquinas because it tells us, more clearly than we can tell ourselves, that there is a sanctity to life that reason cannot touch. And this is his story's lasting lesson: what we know through reason is true, but never enough. That is not a sad lesson, but one of unimaginable joy. We must think of the poor begging friar not as burdened by feelings of despair but as uplifted by a surging wave of contentedness and peace. We must imagine him to be happy.

In a way that not even he, the most articulate of men, could express, Aquinas had broken through to an experience of a reality that was unfathomable. Merely thinking of his experience must move us, as it moved him, to silence. The time for books, the reading and the writing of them, must come to an end. But the silence that falls over us will not be one of defeat or despair. It will be a silence of victory. Not triumphant, not boastful, but a quiet thanksgiving for having reached our journey's end and seen into the invisible heart of all things.

Bound for Heaven

It is no fair criticism of Christianity that not everyone is Christian, just as it is no fair criticism of any faith that not all people profess it. Yet because enlightenment, not religious conversion, is the goal of our inquiry, we can evaluate what Aquinas had to say about happiness quite apart from any requirement of faith or belief. Not everything he said will rise or fall by the truth of Christianity. If Aquinas could hear the voice of truth in Aristotle, perhaps we can hear the same in him.

But what we hear may not be to our liking. The note struck repeatedly throughout Aquinas's writings, and for us it is likely to be clanging and discordant, is that perfect happiness is unattainable in this life. Such a refrain we hear again and again, and never in the quietest tones. This is a too exalted view of happiness, one that does not sit comfortably with our modern belief in self-sufficiency. Why would God create us with the desire to contemplate his essence—the desire hard-wired in our brain, like that for food and shelter and sex—and yet deny us the means to satisfy it?

Heavenly happiness may well be, and certainly Aquinas believed it to be, the enhanced continuation of our earthly happiness. But there is no guarantee that we will end up in heaven. We do not know whether perfect happiness awaits us, nor can we calculate our chances of attaining it because that very attainment lies beyond mortal power. Christianity does provide, through God's grace, the means to achieve perfect happiness, a glimpse of which we can catch here on earth in the kind of breakthrough moment that Aquinas himself experienced. But because we cannot earn or merit grace, we simply have to trust that God will freely and unfailingly bestow it upon us. Surely this is a disdainful view of human life: we can neither renounce our desire for happiness, nor requite it.

And yet to end so discouragingly would be to render falsely Aquinas's vision of happiness. For as much as he insisted on the need for divine grace, and as much as he counseled that reason, however exalted, must be exceeded, he never lost sight of the truth that our search for happiness begins, and must begin, in the practicalities of life. If happiness is an accomplishment, and Aquinas held that it was, then where else would we start to accomplish it than here on earth, in the normal ordinary events that fill our days?

Of all the lessons that the Catholic saint learned from the pagan Greek philosopher, maybe the most surprising one (surprising because *we* have tended to forget it) is that what is most authentic about humanity is the union of body and soul. In a way that defies all subsequent caricature, Aquinas did not regard the body as the root of all evil, the locus of shame. Christ himself was the Word made *flesh*. On his deathbed, Aquinas (himself a sometime poet) called for the Song of Solomon to be read to him. An astonishing choice: at the moment he was about to relinquish his body he wanted nothing so much as to hear a love poem, and thus be reminded of the body's delights. There can be no surer sign than this that our supreme happiness, although it must transcend the world, can never renounce it. The path to happiness may well take us deep into a mystery whose resolution lies in a sphere beyond our immediate reach, but that path is open to all, even to the dumbest ox.

6

THE ALCHEMY OF HAPPINESS
(ISLAM)

An Islamic tradition (*hadith*) states that at the start of every century God sends someone to revitalize and inspire the community of the faithful. The great reformer of the fifth century of the Islamic era was Abu Hamid al-Ghazali (A.D. 1058–1111), the Proof of Islam, the Ornament of Faith, and the Renewer of Religion. Ghazali believed that God had called him to renew Islam in its moment of crisis, and for many Muslims his authority is second only to that of the Prophet Muhammad. He must be counted as one of the most original spiritual thinkers of any culture in any age.

Born in the Persian city of Tûs, in the northeast province of Khorasan, Ghazali demonstrated an early passion for knowledge. "To thirst after a comprehension of things as they really are," he recalled in his spiritual autobiography, *Deliverance from Evil*, "was my habit and custom from a very early age."[1] An encounter with thieves showed the force of that habit, for he demanded that they return, not his money nor his clothes, but only his notebooks. Struck by the boy's audacity, or perhaps just recognizing the limited resale value of a student's scribbling, the thieves handed them over. (On the shrewd presumption that such an appeal was unlikely to elicit a similarly enlightened response from other highwaymen, Ghazali spent the next three years memorizing the contents of those recovered books.) The story is almost certainly fabricated, but it does make the point that Ghazali was someone who desired to know everything. The problem, as he soon discovered, was that he was going about it the wrong way.

As a young man he went on to study law and theology at the Nizamiyya college in Nishapur, where his talents destined him for an academic career. In 1091, only thirty-three years old, he was appointed professor of law at the Nizamiyya college in Baghdad, one of a number of advanced schools established by Nizam al-Mulk, the vizier of the Turkish sultan, to promote Sunni (orthodox) Islam. Ghazali was now a man of high mark and repute.

Shortly after reaching this position of intellectual eminence, he fell victim to a debilitating spiritual crisis. Although never for a moment doubting his faith, Ghazali wondered, nonetheless, whether the lamp of reason could illuminate it. In a way that anticipated Thomas Aquinas, Ghazali believed that reason and faith were partners in the search for ultimate and final truth. So he resolved to search for knowledge beyond doubt and truth beyond corruption. He sought a rational certainty so strong, so steadfast, that not even miracles—the suspension of reason—could overthrow it. But as he found out, the rational mind alone cannot uncover the ultimate truth of things, for there are truths the mind can scarcely imagine, let alone apprehend.

It was during his spiritual crisis that Ghazali became acquainted with Sufism, the mystical side of Islam. Mystics were men not of theories and abstractions, nor of tradition and custom; they were, rather, men of pure experience. And they proved to be a model for Ghazali in his moment of crisis: "I apprehended clearly that the mystics were men who had real experiences, not men of words, and that I had already progressed as far as was possible by way of intellectual apprehension. What remained for me was not to be attained by oral instruction and study but only by immediate experience and by walking in the mystic way."[2]

Setting out on the mystic road to happiness, Ghazali examined his own life. Although his faith in God was sincere, he was ashamed of his attachment to worldly success, his pride, and his hunger for public recognition and esteem. For a time, he lived in fear and indecision. He would awake with a clear resolve to leave Baghdad and forsake his profession, yet by nightfall the morning's confidence had vanished; his faith beckoned him to seek a new life, but the chains of worldly desire held him back. Ghazali could not bring himself to heed the cry of the voice—his own inner voice—that called out to him: "To the road! To the road! What is left of life is but little and the journey before you is long. . . . If you do not prepare *now* for eternal life, when will you prepare? If you do not now sever these attachments, when will you sever them?"[3]

The more Ghazali resisted the call, the more agonizing his crisis became. Broken and exhausted, he finally accepted that only God could heal him. So, at the height of his fame, Ghazali renounced everything that he had struggled so hard to acquire. He told his friends that he was making a pilgrimage to Mecca, but that was just to throw them off the scent; he was actually going to Syria and wanted to make the journey alone. In his heart he vowed to live the life of a poor Sufi mystic, intent on purging his soul of vices, adorning it with virtue, and, ultimately, losing himself in the loving contemplation of God.

When Ghazali left Baghdad, he is said to have taken two mules, both laden with books. Shortly after beginning his journey, robbers sprang upon him. This time, Ghazali was not so persuasive: the thieves overpowered him and made off with every last book. Some years later, in Mecca, after he had experienced an inner awakening, the immortal Sufi guide Khidr appeared to him in a vision. He told Ghazali that if the books had *not* been stolen he would have remained enslaved to them, and so would never have read the book of true knowledge within his own heart.

Khidr provided the mystic interpretation of the event, revealing the deeper truth under the surface of mere circumstance. No doubt the tales of Ghazali and the book thieves are apocryphal (like so many anecdotes in Sufi texts) for their primary purpose is symbolic: to reveal a hidden meaning. Through the two stories we learn that there is a time for us to follow the path of reason and, equally, a time to depart from it. Wisdom lies in knowing when the time has come for us to leave reason behind.

Without his books, but with more wisdom, Ghazali settled in Damascus, where he spent two peaceful years in reflection and religious devotion. In the streets and marketplaces of Damascus it would have been difficult for someone of Ghazali's stature to remain completely anonymous, so he must have welcomed the chance to pass his days in undisturbed solitude. He put that solitude to good use, for through the habit of meditation he recovered from his spiritual crisis. The recovery came not through his own power, but through (to use his favorite metaphor) the light of God shining into his heart. God's pure gift to a sinful mankind, this light penetrates our soul and pierces our heart with such force that, as Ghazali taught, we have no choice but to renounce this world of illusion and turn our entire being toward the one true reality that is God.

After achieving this state of enlightenment, Ghazali returned to the world. He traveled first to Jerusalem, where he prayed at the Dome of the Rock, the site of Solomon's temple and, according to tradition, Abraham's sacrifice of his son Isaac and Muhammad's miraculous night journey to heaven. Ghazali then embarked on a pilgrimage to Mecca—thus fulfilling one of the requirements of traditional Islamic law (the *sharia*)—a trip that also allowed him to pray at the tombs of Abraham in Hebron and Muhammad in Medina. Only after visiting

Mecca did he return to Baghdad, where he was reunited with his children. He eventually moved back to Tûs, his birthplace, where he founded a monastic religious community.

What Ghazali learned in his period of solitude he recorded in his greatest work, *The Revival of the Religious Sciences (Ihya 'Ulum ad-Din)*, which runs to six thousand pages across four massive volumes. (It was publicly burned in Muslim Spain before Ghazali became a great religious authority.) Later, he prepared a greatly condensed version of his Arabic masterpiece for the benefit of common readers (people like us today), who needed spiritual wisdom and moral guidance just as much as the religious elite. Ghazali was careful to write this more popular book in Persian, the vernacular tongue of his countrymen. He called it *The Alchemy of Happiness (Kimiya-i-Sa'adat)*.

Before long, Ghazali was enticed back into the lecture hall at the Nizamiyya college in Nishapur, where he had studied in his youth. He returned to his profession a changed man:

> I had been disseminating the knowledge by which worldly success is attained. . . . But now I am calling men to the knowledge whereby worldly success is given up and its low position in the scale of real worth is recognized. This is now my intention, my aim, my desire; God knows that this is so. It is my earnest longing that I may make myself and others better. I do not know whether I shall reach my goal or whether I shall be taken away while short of my object.[4]

In one of history's sad ironies, Ghazali was taken away from this noble task only a few years later. On the morning of his death, before first light, he asked for a shroud. He kissed it and laid it over his eyes, saying, "Obediently I enter into the presence of the King." He stretched out his feet and turned to face Mecca. By sunrise, he was dead.

The Journey Inward

At the heart of Islam lies the Koran, the sacred text that God revealed to the Prophet Muhammad in the cave on Mount Hira around the year 610. The Koran, which embodies the full range of principles and values by which Muslims are called to order their lives, is supplemented by the Prophet's many sayings and reports of his actions and decisions. Together, these texts shape the Muslim tradition known as the Prophetic Way (*al-Sunnah*). This tradition, like that of the other monotheistic faiths, centers on laws to be obeyed, commandments to be fulfilled, and rules to be correctly followed.

Yet the "religions of the book" have another side, a side that reveals their inner meaning. This further, hidden dimension is mysticism. Not so much a school of thought, mysticism is more an attitude or way of life because it seeks to penetrate through a religion's outward form to find its deeper truth—a truth that cannot be expressed in normal thought and language. Mysticism in all religions has certain shared characteristics. Above all, it is a personal experience, and not a general theory or abstract idea; it requires an inward journey (frequently symbolized as an outward ascent); and it depends not on logic, but on imagination. In the modern West, mysticism is often misunderstood as self-indulgent, or bundled together with a vague New Age spiritualism, itself a descendant of the 1960s hippie counterculture. All that confusion makes it difficult for us to appreciate the insight and rigor of this ancient and extraordinary spiritual path.

Heirs as we are to the rational traditions of science and logic, we might greet with skepticism, perhaps ridicule, the mystic's claim that imagination is the path to happiness. But imagination is not alien to reason. (How else do scientific discoveries occur except when scientists *imagine* that something is true—the hypothesis—and then set about to prove it?) Imagination is not about making things up—that is fantasy, which is something entirely different—but about grasping truths that lie beyond our rational comprehension. Through the gateway of imagination, we gain access to what is absent, what is not in view, what is, at least for now, only a possibility. Can we really be surprised that it takes some imagination to be happy? Your happiness must, to some extent, be found in a realm beyond reason because it begins with imagining a future reality: the self that you might become.

And so mysticism requires intense imaginative experiences not for any gratuitous reason, but for the legitimate one that it aims at a truth that cannot be put into mere words. Because, by definition, an infinite God is incommensurate with finite human beings, we cannot know God directly; our sense perceptions and rational thoughts will be of no help. Any argument that the human mind can devise for the existence of God is pointless, because wherever God exists, it is in a realm beyond our mind's comprehension. Whoever God is, he is a being beyond logic, which is why science can neither prove nor disprove his existence. Yet if we cannot think of God, still we can *imagine* him. Through myths, symbols, and archetypes, we can touch on a reality that we cannot fully grasp. True, we create such images with our mind, but we *feel* a deeper dimension within them. We intuit a secret meaning that reason cannot disclose.

Prescribed rules of conduct, the great mystics of all faiths have always believed, are of only limited value in our search for happiness— or the quest for the ground of all being, or the contemplation of God's essence, to state it more theologically. Indeed, at some point such rules might need to be set aside so that individual mystic experience can take the precedence it deserves. "The enlightened man," Ghazali wrote, "knows, not by hearsay or traditional belief, but by actual experience, what produces wretchedness or happiness in the soul."[5]

Eastern religions have been the most accepting of mysticism precisely because they are not so caught up in rules and commandments. In walking the mystic way, they have less baggage to leave behind. By contrast, the conforming rituals and traditions of Islam, Christianity, and Judaism have always been at odds with openness to the power of personal experience. And yet even there, in such seemingly infertile soil, mysticism has taken root. In the history of Islam, it was mystic thought—Sufism—that gave exuberance and freedom to a tradition that had come to seem rigid and locked.

Ah, Sweet Mystery

Sufism holds that Islam has two aspects: outward form and inner spirit. (The name is thought to derive from *suf*, the white woolen robe that Muslim mystics have worn for more than a thousand years and that is said to have been favored by the Prophet himself.) It emerged within decades of Muhammad's lifetime as a reaction against unduly literal adherence to the laws and forms of Islamic religious culture. By protesting against an exactitude that threatened to reduce their religion to mere blind obedience to rituals and commandments, the Sufis challenged anyone who had accepted Islamic law in a merely superficial way—the outward form—to discover its deep and rich inner meaning. They did not want to overturn religious law so much as they wanted to enrich the understanding of it.

The distinction that the Sufis made between the outward form of religious ritual and its inward aspect is not a cryptic one, for we all easily understand the difference between form and content, appearance and substance, exterior and interior. Take the example of the five daily prayers that every Muslim is called on to recite. These ritual actions possess both a surface form and a deep content. Turning to face Mecca when you pray is the outward sign of turning your heart toward

God. Similarly, the requirement to purify the site where you pray is the symbol of purifying your heart.

On a grander scale, the pilgrimage to Mecca represents, in its outward form, travel to the world's holiest site. The inner meaning is that you must travel away from your sins, leaving behind your old self: the *real* pilgrimage is an inward moral journey. The visible actions of prayer and pilgrimage, far from being mere formalities, are charged with symbolic force and remind us of an invisible meaning; without that meaning, the actions are hollow and empty. Performing a religious ritual in a mechanical way, without purity of intention, is mere pretense, and so does not help us to move closer to God. It is not enough to do the right thing; we must do it for the right reason and in the right spirit.

Every monotheistic religion struggles with the tensions that inevitably arise between those who emphasize outward form and those who search for inner meaning. By Ghazali's day, nearly five hundred years after the revelation of the Koran, Islam was threatened by an ever-widening rift between Sufism and orthodox faith. The Sufis were denounced for placing personal experience above religious law, thus allowing themselves (allegedly) to justify any action, however sinful, by claiming that it was divinely inspired. Traditional theologians, meanwhile, were criticized for draining Islam of its vitality and passion, for reducing it to a dutiful but unthinking compliance with rules. It was Ghazali's mission to reconcile these seemingly opposing forces.

Like the Sufi mystic Abu'l-Qasim al-Junayd (d. 910), in whose footsteps he followed, Ghazali believed that mystical knowledge must have boundaries, and that those boundaries were not arbitrary but firmly set by the Koran and the Traditions. Extreme mysticism would harm the Muslim community by encouraging vanity and the neglect of useful labor. If every farmer gave up farming to pursue mystic ecstasy, Ghazali prudently advised, then no one would be left to keep the world going. Yet he also affirmed (though never himself experiencing it) the reality of the mystical union between God and man. We should imagine Ghazali weaving a mystic thread into the whole cloth of Islam, drawing together and uniting what only appeared to be conflicting ideas and beliefs. (The search for common ground is, of course, how *all* societies, Eastern and Western, ancient and modern, solve their problems.)

Moreover, Ghazali's own life is a living symbol of the Sufi path and its integration of outer form and inner reality. Throughout his youth, and until his spiritual crisis, Ghazali had focused entirely on Islam's outer form: the careful study of its laws and the dutiful observance of its rituals. But after his conversion to Sufism, he gained a mystical insight into the deeper truth that could scarcely be expressed in any outward, material way. During his years of prayerful solitude and wandering he cultivated this new experience of entering more profoundly, more soulfully, into prophetic revelation. The culminating moment, the moment of integration, came in the last years of his life, when he returned home to teach. As Ghazali was careful to point out, his return to his birthplace was not a simple going back to the way things had been previously, because he himself was now transformed. Because he had been transformed he could guide others to the truth that he had at last realized.

Ghazali was particularly struck by the story of Junayd reproaching a novice for shrieking ecstatically while listening to music during a Sufi assembly. After a period of self-imposed restraint, the youth's pent-up emotions became so intense that he uttered one last shriek and died on the spot. In one sense, the story conveys the paradoxical truth (as expressed in the hadith "Die before you die") that in life you must die to your false self and be reborn as your true self. This is a fundamental Sufi principle, and we shall soon come back to it. In a cautionary sense, though, the story of the shrieking novice reminds us that

extreme outward expressions of mystical understanding can be fraudulent or counterfeit. Irrational behavior does not, in itself, express anything other than a refusal to be rational. In most cases, reason is a
trustworthy guide, and we ignore its counsel to our cost.

But reason will have its limits, for although it can be used in infinite
ways—we can always find something new to think about—it can give
us knowledge only of finite things: a thunderstorm, a chemical reaction,
a legal principle. By definition, reason cannot know, except through
vague, speculative analogy, what lies beyond its borders. A few centuries
after Ghazali, the mystic poet Shabistari (c. 1250–1320) took up the
theme of reason's blindness in his poem "The Secret Rose Garden":

> As the man blind from birth
> Believes not nor understands
> Your description of colours,
> Even if you showed him proofs for a century,
> So blind reason cannot see the future state.
> But beyond reason man has a certain knowledge
> Which God has placed in his soul and body
> Whereby he perceives the hidden mysteries.[6]

To see the future state and to perceive the hidden mysteries is a privilege that belongs only to a special class of people—prophets, saints,
and great spiritual teachers—who transcend reason through a holy,
prophetic spirit. Some of us will doubt that such a prophetic spirit
exists because we have no experience of it. (Indeed, very few of us will
ever experience it.) But that, Ghazali insisted, is as absurd as the tone-
deaf man who declares that there is no such thing as music just because
he himself cannot hear it. We may not deny the truth of mysticism just
because we ourselves have not received it. If we have doubts, let us be
generous enough to imagine a knowledge that exceeds reason. Such

knowledge can lead to a direct experience of God, which explains why Ghazali called true mystics "those who have arrived": they are completely absorbed within the supreme being and are at one with its unity. They have arrived at the summit of comprehension and know all that there is to be known.

Disappointingly, few among us will transcend reason, at least here on earth. To illustrate the difference between the many (who are bound by reason's shackle) and the few (who break free of it), Ghazali used the image of a nut. Just as a nut comprises an outer husk, an inner rind, a kernel, and the precious oil extracted from the kernel, religious believers are similarly varied. The husk represents those who profess belief but lack conviction, and so their faith exists on the surface level; the inner rind stands for all those who have a sincere faith, but one they have accepted on mere hearsay from parents and teachers; the kernel signifies those who have a more personal faith but are still attached to the world; the oil extracted from the kernel symbolizes something truly rare: the mystic whose faith is pure, in the same way that almond oil is the pure essence of the almond.

Most of us, said Ghazali, will never get beyond the inner rind. In other words, although everyone is called to observe religious law, only a few will penetrate to the law's inner meaning and thus apprehend the mystic virtues. Only to these devout few is the mystic way open, and only they can reorient their lives in pursuit of the more exalted virtues that contain the hidden meaning of the lower ones.

Beyond the Mountains

Mystics in all traditions, not just Islam, describe their experience as following a path. Frequently, this path is vertical, an ascent, to emphasize that the mystic strives for improvement, moral refinement, and the apprehension of higher truths. The path is a path to be climbed, for it begins with the lower self but ends in union with God, the highest reality. The upward journey is arduous, and like a mountain climber struggling to reach the next crevice or ledge on the rocky surface, we struggle to acquire virtue in the midst of life's harshness.

Many passages from the Koran hold a mystical significance for Sufis; in such passages they find hidden, esoteric meanings about the nature of the path or ascent. It is not difficult to imagine studying the Koran for secret meanings since it was traditionally committed to memory (especially at a time when literacy was not widespread) and then recited, both silently and aloud. The Koran was ever present in the believer's mind—living inside one's head, so to speak—and thus a constant source of inspiration. Passages that might be passed over in reading could be dwelt on at length through memory, fueling the imagination and giving rise to ever deeper and more complex interpretations.

The Sufis were inspired by the story of Muhammad's mystical ascent to heaven and regarded it as a founding example of the Sufi path and a model for religious seekers throughout the ages. One night, while in a meditative trance, the Prophet was carried on the back of a winged horse called Buraq, first to the ruined Temple of Solomon in Jerusalem (where he prayed with the prophets Abraham, Moses, and Jesus) and then upward to the Seventh Heaven. The site of the ascent is marked by the Dome of the Rock, the holiest shrine in Islam outside Mecca. Symbolically, the heavenward ascent stands for the journey of humanity to its outermost limit, where it stands on the threshold of transcendent reality and final meaning. It signifies that worldly attachments—and more than that, worldly experiences and ways of understanding—have been left far behind. To describe the ascent in words is already to betray it, to create a false rendering, because the experience itself surpasses the boundaries of human language. Words can only fail to convey the highest reality.

And yet we must make do with words, for that is all we have. We need not despair, however, because poetry has long been a way for words to hint at something beyond themselves, some dimension of truth that they cannot fully capture but only latch onto for a fleeting moment. So when the Sufis wanted to describe the mystical ascent, they used a language of symbols and images. In the West, the most widely known work of Sufi poetry is *The Rubaiyat of Omar Khayyam* ("A loaf of bread, a jug of wine, and thou"). But if you want to discover the greatest allegorical expression of the Sufi path, you must turn to an epic poem of five thousand lines written in the twelfth century by another Persian writer, the sometime pharmacist Fariduddin Attar. This inspirational classic is called *The Conference of the Birds*. It is no accident that the story is about birds, for the bird is an ancient symbol of the human soul, which can be either caged or set free.

As the poem begins, the birds of the world realize that they are the only creatures who lack a supreme ruler, and so they decide to search for one. They elect a hoopoe bird to guide them in their quest. The hoopoe is no ordinary bird, for he had been entrusted by King Solomon to carry messages to the Queen of Sheba. On his head he bears a crest of feathers to signify his attainment of spiritual wisdom, and on his beak is written the word *Bismillah* ("in the name of God"), the first word of the Koran. The hoopoe symbolizes our need for the guidance of a spiritual master (*shaykh*) as we make our inner journey to enlightenment and happiness.

Assuming his role as guide and mentor, the hoopoe warns the other birds that their journey will be arduous and long. More encouragingly, he also tells them that the journey will be worthwhile because the birds *do* have a king. His name is Simurgh, and he lives at the end of the world, beyond the mountains of Kaf. To reach their mysterious king, the birds must pass through seven valleys, each with its own dangers. At first, the birds rejoice, but some of them quickly succumb to despair and doubt. A few back out of the journey before it begins, protesting that it will be too difficult, or that finding their king doesn't really matter to them. The nightingale is the first to refuse, as he cannot bear to be parted from his beloved, the rose. The hawk decides to stay the servant of its royal master, and the duck is content to paddle away in the river.

The reluctant birds represent those of us who are so attached to worldly goods that we cannot even begin our spiritual journey, let alone awaken to a higher reality. Like the nightingale, we mistake the passing beauty of the world for God's eternal beauty; like the hawk, we mistake humans' temporal authority for God's everlasting rule. And just as the duck proudly swears that he is clean because he spends all his time in water, we delude ourselves into believing that our souls are already pure, and so we need make no more effort. In the birds' unwillingness to embark on the journey you are meant to see the reflection of your own anxieties and fears about the path to inner wisdom. Part of you wants to set out on this path, for you yearn (as we all do) to be united with something greater than yourself. Yet another part of you, the weaker part, shrinks back in fear, knowing that to complete the journey you must abandon all the things that seem most precious to you. You must risk everything, and you worry that you might lose it.

Not all the birds, however, are scared, and the resolute ones begin the journey. Some falter along the way, and to embolden them the hoopoe tells stories of what they can expect in each of the seven valleys. After many years, they pass through the valleys and finally reach Simurgh's palace. Only thirty birds remain. The seven valleys are the seven steps along the Sufi path, or the ascending stages of the soul as it progresses toward perfect happiness. They include the renunciation of worldly goods, detachment from desire, and the recognition of the unity of all things. In more modern idiom, we could say that the valleys represent moments of greater and greater enlightenment of our consciousness.

Has the journey been worth the effort? And just who is Simurgh, the king that the thirty birds have sought? The answer lies within the name itself, for in Persian *simurgh* means "thirty birds." (For the Sufis, wordplay is not a trick, but a means of conveying a true yet secret meaning.) When the thirty birds finally enter the palace to meet their true king, they discover, to their astonishment, that they themselves are Simurgh:

> There in the Simurgh's radiant face they saw
> Themselves, the Simurgh of the world—with awe
> They gazed, and dared at last to comprehend
> They were the Simurgh and the journey's end.[7]

The moment when the birds look at their king and see themselves staring back is a moment not of selfish arrogance, but its opposite: the absorption of the self into the fullest reality. That is the moment, so longed for, of spiritual awakening and the realization of a deeper, more profound reality within this life. Like the thirty birds, we, too, can penetrate to the heart of things, to the essence of truth, and see cosmic unity everywhere, including within ourselves. Parallels to other religious traditions spring immediately to mind, whether the profound silence that overtook Aquinas in his final days or the Hindu teaching that ultimate reality is everywhere, like a grain of salt dissolved in water.

Attar's poem is enchanting and entertaining, but that is not its purpose. Its purpose is to illuminate, to show us a picture of life more penetratingly real than could be achieved through book learning and cold logic. The story of the birds should spark within you a lightning flash of intuitive insight, the merest beginning of mystical perception. The poem's value lies not in the story that it tells but in the strength of your response to it. Like all Sufi poetry it was intended to be recited, and you must listen out of longing for contact with something greater, not a desire for pleasure or amusement. You listen to the poet's words, but what you hear—with the ear of your heart—is the voice of God.

Overcoming the Self

As the birds near the end of their long journey, they ask the hoopoe what gift they should give to Simurgh. He tells them to present the king with something that cannot be found in his court. What could that be, the birds wonder, for surely so great a king lacks for nothing. Not so, says the hoopoe; there are two things unknown in Simurgh's realm: a heart filled with longing and a soul in torment.

The lesson for us is clear: we embark on the mystic path not because we are strong, and thus can endure it, but because we are weak, and thus need it. The inward journey arises out of our weakness, out of our desire to overcome the lack within us. Paradoxically, these negative and empty and unwelcome feelings are precisely what make us poised for happiness. For only by acknowledging the deficit in our soul can we ever move beyond it.

Our desire to move beyond our limitations leads on to the story's deeper lesson: that we are captive to a false sense of identity and must overcome it in order to arrive at our true self. The great Sufi poet Jalal al-Din Rumi (1207–1273) wrote, in a way that at first seems puzzling, about the need to die to ourselves in order to become truly ourselves:

> *I, being self-confined,*
> *Self did not merit,*
> *Till, leaving self behind,*
> *Did self inherit.*[8]

As Rumi tells us, the egoistic manner in which we are conditioned, or accustomed, to understand ourselves ("being self-confined") is illusory, although to us it does not seem that way. Indeed, the illusion seems the most real thing we know. But that is only because we have not yet gained the wisdom to see beyond it. We are like the dreamer who mistakes the dream for reality: the actual reality is there all the time, but we have not yet woken up to it.

At the risk, perhaps, of some confusion, we could say that the self is the self's problem. Or, to put it in modern psychoanalytic terms, the *ego* is the self's problem. We have seen this before, most vividly in the Buddhist belief that the ego is a trap, and that the defensive project of our self-image needs to be dismantled. In a similar way, Sufi mystics believe that the problem self—the unhappy self—is the one enslaved by desire and governed by base instincts and appetites. They teach that although we know (and have known all along) what is right, we keep inclining toward the wrong, like a ship that has lost its moorings.

Yet even in that bewildered state, so the mystics assure us, we perceive, however dimly, that something is amiss, that somehow this accustomed self is inauthentic and needs correction. Sensing the falseness within, we yearn for truth to take its place. We feel our own insincerity as a deep and festering wound, the wound of absence. Yet this act of self-reproach—the heart filled with longing, the soul in torment, the unhappy self—is precisely what gets us on our way. From the wreck of reproach we salvage hope. Dismayed though we are by our current self, we know that we are but the prelude to an eventually transformed self. Who you *would* be, you *can* be.

It is difficult to express in a literal way what it means to overcome yourself, to deflate your ego. Buddha likened it to a flame that has been extinguished. For Aquinas, it was the realization that all his writings were no better than straw. The Sufi poet Attar expressed it as the birds' recognition that they themselves were "the Simurgh of the world." The mutual identity shared by Simurgh and the thirty birds, which makes them in some way indivisible, reveals one of Sufism's core principles: that you can be united with a reality beyond yourself.

In trying to express this ineffable truth, Sufi writers have used other images: a river that empties into the ocean, a spark that shoots out of a flame and then falls back into it. The poet Rumi wrote of the reed flute, cut from the reed bed, whose plaintive sound expresses its yearning to return home. In the song of the flute we hear the cry of our lost unhappy souls. These are powerful ancient metaphors of our healing journey back toward the divine creator from whom we have been separated.

The Alchemy of Happiness

Perhaps the greatest lesson we can learn from the Sufis is that whether we realize it or not, we are all searching for what is absent in our lives, dimly aware that we have been cut off from the origin of our being. Thus, being in God's presence, beholding his face, is, for the Sufis, the supreme pleasure and ultimate end of human life. That is also what Aquinas meant when he wrote that happiness is contemplating the beatific vision. Whereas Christianity teaches that perfect happiness exists only in heaven, Islam teaches that a direct encounter with God's essence can occur during a lifetime—but that such a supreme experience is granted only to the prophets, the saints, and the Sufi masters.

Though you and I will probably never reach the higher mystical states, the mere awareness of their existence can help us to refocus our lives in a more honest way, to begin working on the self-transformation that Ghazali called "the alchemy of happiness." The name Ghazali, in some variants, means "the spinner," and it is tempting to read it as yet another symbol of self-transformation. Like the spinner who turns raw materials into something finished and fine, the spiritual teacher Ghazali takes coarse humanity and spins it into a state of moral refinement.

Because the Sufi path awakens us to an *inner* reality, there is always the risk that aspirants will misinterpret that reality because they are unprepared for it, or will succumb to emotional hysteria and self-delusion. As a safeguard, the aspirant entrusts himself to a spiritual teacher in a Sufi order to oversee the process of his transformation. Under the teacher's guidance, the novice stays true to the path and does not lead himself into error. The Sufi orders, which arose in the twelfth century, are not monastic orders, such as found in Christianity, but fellowships, or confraternities, of those who have chosen to follow the Sufi path. Each order has developed a particular outward form of undertaking the inner journey, a particular set of actions that elicit an ecstatic response—a state of exaltation—which brings the Sufi closer to God's presence.

The most famous of the Sufi orders is the Mevlevi, whose members are known throughout the West as the whirling dervishes because of the distinctive dance they perform as a means of concentration. (The dervishes spend 1,001 days learning the dance by spinning around a large nail placed between the first two toes of the left foot.) As they become absorbed in the spinning motion of the dance, the dervishes feel the boundaries of the self begin to melt away. The dancers wear black cloaks that they cast off, revealing white garments underneath. The symbolism is far from obscure: the dance is a mystical journey from the death of the self to resurrection in union with God. It is something more than a cliché to state that the dervishes lose themselves in the dance.

For Westerners particularly it is easy to be distracted by the exoticism of the Sufi orders, especially when they are as thrilling as the whirling dervishes. But nothing would be a greater betrayal of Sufism than to focus exclusively on the outward form of its practices—the dancing, the spinning, the howling—for that is to neglect the inner meaning. Silence, just as much as frenzy, can be a sign of mystic insight, a way of experiencing transcendent happiness here on earth (as Aquinas, in his final days, must surely have known). Such has been the teaching of the great Sufi masters for the past thousand years. Always, your goal must be what lies underneath the world of appearance, what is largely hidden from view.

The stages of the Sufi path vary according to the teacher (who recognizes that each of us must walk his or her own path), but they always begin with repentance and culminate in an emptying of the self so that it can be absorbed in a reunion with God. What all the paths and all the mystic teachings have in common is the quest for unity and the soul's desire to find happiness by merging with something beyond itself. We can feel this call for unity most powerfully in the emotional extravagance of Sufi poetry. Drunkenness is the most unlikely, and yet the most suggestive, image of spiritual ecstasy and the joy of being united with God. But more important than euphoria is the altered state of consciousness, the slipping away of the self, when we are absorbed into the divine unity. Just as the drunkard loses self-control—his speech is slurred, his movements shaky and unbalanced—the mystic gradually surrenders his ego, allowing the self to be annihilated.

The great Sufi poets are not teaching that intoxication is the path to wisdom and happiness; rather, they are speaking figuratively, using words to express a truth that words cannot adequately convey. All mystic poetry relies on this sort of negative aesthetic, for it reaches out to something beyond itself, something that language can only hint at. Paradoxically, then, the true meaning of Sufi poetry lies in what the words *fail* to say. As the medieval poet Shabistari put it:

> *Within the mere words and sounds*
> *Of the mystic song*
> *Lies a precious mystery.*[9]

For some of us, however, the precious mystery will remain a mystery. We hear the poet's words but are deaf to their meaning. How can we talk about mysticism in a world that is not prepared for it? Spiritual states are visible in ways that are easily misunderstood: ecstatic utterances, wild movements, or fixed trances. When the "drunken" mystic Bayazid (d. 875) exclaimed "Glory be to me!" he was accused of blasphemy because the literal meaning of his words was offensive to his fellow Muslims: he made a god of himself. Yet such utterances cannot be understood literally, but only metaphorically. To those who cannot appreciate them in this way, mystic insights will seem at best mere nonsense, at worst the dangerous doings of a heretic.

And yet mystic visions are as real as the things we experience in the world, but real in a different way. The reality they disclose cannot be demonstrated through scientific experiment, but only perceived by the imagination. Thus, for the mystic, a vision that he or she creates is an earthly manifestation of a truth that exists more perfectly in the divine sphere. Neither indulging a fantasy nor telling a lie, the mystic conjures up in this world something that originates in an immaterial, transcendent realm.

If interpreted literally, Sufi poetry and ecstatic practices will confuse, perhaps threaten, anyone who does not possess the knowledge or disposition necessary to understand their symbolic force. Not everyone is prepared to find ultimate truth—or happiness, or enlightenment—through his or her own imagination. Often, we simply want to be told—first by parents and teachers, and later by superiors and authority figures—what is true, what is right, and what to believe. What we don't want is to doubt or to ask questions or to live with uncertainty. So to anyone who blindly accepts a secondhand faith, mere hearsay, the mystic path will seem strewn with error.

As Junayd understood, it is dangerous to speak of such things too loudly, too openly, because other people—the uninitiated—are bound to misunderstand them, and that could lead to suspicion and alarm. Because spiritual states are essentially private, it is impossible for anyone on the outside to enter into that experience. Nobody but you can really know what is happening inside you. And so even to write about the mystic search for happiness, particularly in a general sense (as I have been doing), is already to depart from it, already to slant it in a misleading way. Sufism is really not something that you (or anyone) can learn about; it is something that you must experience from the inside.

"A walnut for everyone who slaps me"

On first acquaintance, mysticism has a surprisingly modern feel. It values personal experience, expresses the freedom of the individual, and looks suspiciously on all things regimented and doctrinaire. It sits harmoniously with our reigning desire to be liberated. This may well explain why, nearly a thousand years after Ghazali wrote it, *The Alchemy of Happiness* still strikes a chord with readers, including—especially—those in the secular West. Yet, in other respects, the mystic path to happiness is not easy to understand, let alone follow. It does not conform to our rational, empirical mind-set; it presumes that everyone believes in a God; it takes long periods of training and apprenticeship. In a quick-fix culture, the patient nurturing of insight into a higher reality will scarcely seem worth the effort. We want happiness, but we want it now.

Despite suspiciously easy parallels with New Age seekers, mysticism (of whatever origin) must strike us as the invention of an alien culture: one that regards people as inherently unequal, at least in terms of their ability to apprehend the fundamental truth of things. The distinction between the ignorant many (and most of us must be included in that group) and the knowledgeable few is the aspect of mysticism most at odds with Western democratic values and an ingrained belief in equality. There is no getting around the uncomfortable fact that the mystic view of happiness is elitist. Not that the mystics try to prevent us from becoming happy, but that true happiness can come only to those select few who are versed in the ways of imagination and intuition. Only they will know the highest form of bliss because only they will know the inner meaning of outward appearance.

It did not bother Ghazali that some people were forever barred from perfect happiness. Otherwise, he would not have told the following story. Bayazid, the famous "drunken" Sufi, was approached by an unhappy man who protested that he had fasted and prayed for thirty years yet was no closer to finding spiritual joy. The mystic told him that not even three hundred years would be time enough. "Why?" the man asked. "Because your selfishness stands between you and God." Desperate, the man pleaded to be taught how to surmount the obstacle of his own selfishness. Bayazid told him that there was indeed a way forward, but it would be impossible to follow. The man insisted that he be told. Relenting, Bayazid commanded him to shave his beard, wear only a loincloth, put on a feeding bag full of walnuts, and then stand in the marketplace, shouting "A walnut for everyone who slaps me." If he could do that, then he might find some happiness. The man scoffed at the suggestion, just as Bayazid knew he would. And yet, as the Sufi master added, there was no other way.

We are the man who refuses to stand in the marketplace and be slapped. Like him, we cannot imagine how to become happy. And imagination is the secret. When the path to happiness is laid out for us, we reject it as ridiculous and humiliating. We turn our backs on it. It seems to be not within our power to move from ignorance to knowledge, from misery to happiness.

But perhaps that is too darkly pessimistic a view. We cannot all be mystics, nor would all of us want to be, but we can try to preserve and honor something of mysticism's spirit in our lives. We can begin to see through this hazy world of appearances into a deeper and clearer reality. The deeds of Ghazali, the sublime verse of medieval Islamic poets, and the arresting practices of Sufi disciples still hold the power to inspire. Such things are not cold to the touch. We cannot know of them and remain unmoved. Even if all we take away from them is a glimmering of some greater happiness, still that may be enough—for a glimmering is a hopeful promise of what is yet to come.

PART IV

Enduring Suffering

7

IT'S ALL IN YOUR MIND
(THE STOICS)

A man with a broken leg is a natural Stoic. In 1992, Admiral James B. Stockdale came to national attention when he was named Ross Perot's running mate on the Reform Party ticket in that year's presidential election. (At the polls, Bill Clinton ousted the incumbent, George H. W. Bush.) An unwilling aspirant to national office, Stockdale (who died in July 2005) was, by temperament and appearance, ill-suited for the slick media exchanges that pass for political discourse today. On screens throughout the country he came across as precisely the man he was: a cantankerous, white-haired sea dog who walked with a pronounced limp.

The limp resulted from an old war injury. During the Vietnam War, Stockdale was a carrier-based fighter pilot with the Navy, in command of Air Wing 16. Since the start of the war he had flown nearly two hundred successful combat missions south of Hanoi. But on the 9th of September 1965, his luck ran out. When he piloted his A-4 Skyraider off the flight deck of the USS *Oriskany* he little suspected that it would be his final mission over North Vietnam. Pulling out of his dive after bombing a cargo train, he was shot down by enemy anti-aircraft fire. He parachuted out of his plane and broke his leg as he fell to the ground.

On landing, he was beaten by villagers and then taken prisoner by North Vietnamese soldiers. Along with the ten other members of his crew, he remained their captive for eight years in Hoa Lo Prison, the infamous Hanoi Hilton. As Stockdale explains in his memoirs, his captors were experts in torture: they beat and whipped him, nearly choked him to death with ropes, chained him in leg irons, denied him access to medical care, and refused to give him letters from home. The torments would stop, he was told, if he went on television to condemn the war and denounce his country's political establishment. Though he suffered greatly, Stockdale refused to break. During the first few years of his imprisonment he could not stand upright because of his injured leg. He was forced into solitary confinement—not just alone, but in total darkness—for four years, during which time he communicated with the other American prisoners in adjoining cells by tapping out code on the wall. Far from being broken, Stockdale broke the will of his own tormentors, who at last began to treat their prisoners with something less than cruelty.

Stockdale attributed his survival, both physical and mental, to the teachings of the Stoic philosopher Epictetus (c. A.D. 50–130). When Stockdale was a graduate student at Stanford, his philosophy professor gave him a copy of Epictetus's *Enchiridion,* a short manual on how to lead the Stoic life. At first, the young military officer doubted the value of this collection of ancient philosophical precepts. (Was he not taught that Frederick the Great always went into battle with a copy at his side?) Yet as he lay suffering with a fractured leg, Stockdale drew strength from Epictetus's assertion that "lameness is an impediment to the body but not to the will."[1] This was no abstract principle of the moral imagination issued by someone sheltered from real-life hardship. To the contrary. Epictetus knew what he wrote about: when he was still a servant, his master, in an act of sheer cruelty, broke both his legs, crippling him for life.

The example of Epictetus helped Stockdale to realize the Stoic truth that happiness is the virtue of indifference to whatever is beyond our control. For him, Stoic detachment was uncannily applicable to his own misfortune: his North Vietnamese captors could imprison his body, but never his mind. And as long as he preserved freedom in his mind, he really was free. Physical captivity, however agonizing, could not deprive him of his liberty. The constant and heroic Admiral Stockdale is a humbling modern example of philosophy's ancient power to help us endure unimaginable misery and suffering. Yet it is equally, and encouragingly, true that Stoicism can appeal to us when we suffer in more ordinary ways; when we feel, as so often we do, that the day-to-day struggle just to survive can be affliction enough.

Born in Adversity

As befits a school of thought that helps its adherents to prepare for the worst, Stoicism was born in that most harrowing of circumstances, a shipwreck. Headed elsewhere, the maritime passenger Zeno of Cittium (334–262 B.C.) was forced to land in Athens, a place that evidently earned his loyalty, as he lived there until his death fifty years later. The young man already possessed a spirit of detachment, for on learning that his possessions were lost at sea, he calmly replied, "Fortune bids me be less encumbered." Once settled into Athenian life, the involuntarily unencumbered Zeno began to study philosophy, the city's most celebrated commodity.

No admirer of Epicurus (who had returned to Athens a few years earlier), Zeno believed that happiness should be based on reason, not pleasure. Rejecting the hedonist's obsession with individual desire, he insisted that the wise man was not free to ignore his duties and obligations to others. Living the good life meant throwing yourself into society, however messy and troubling that turned out to be. It was a sign of Zeno's commitment to the general welfare that he taught not in seclusion (as Epicurus did) but in the Stoa Poecile, a public structure that consisted of a long painted colonnade with an adjoining courtyard. Stoicism took its name from this place where Zeno, who preferred colonnades because he had a habit of pacing up and down while teaching, instructed his first pupils.

The Stoic's concern for others made the good life a rather unpredictable affair, because it entailed dealing with the changing, often disordered circumstances of other people's lives. Zeno's followers understood that moral standards could not exist apart from the actual circumstances of everyday life; otherwise, they would not serve their purpose but would be unheeded empty principles. As Stoicism migrated from democratic Athens to republican (and then imperial) Rome, it increasingly adopted this more pragmatic outlook. Stoicism spares no time for us to dwell on our moods or wallow in our feelings because there is urgent business to be done. As a Stoic, you will learn how to cope not just with life's ordinary ups and downs, but with its major traumas: death and bereavement, the loss of status or reputation, and worries about money and health. As well, you will learn how to cope with success, for good fortune carries its own burdens, as any paparazzi-hounded celebrity will plaintively cry.

Although criticized for being more a coping mechanism than a fully articulated philosophy, Stoicism has been the West's most enduring philosophy of consolation. Repudiating the power of a brutal world to make anyone unhappy, Stoicism has always appealed to those who live in dark times. Its lasting influence has been secured not by the totality of its principles (no such totality exists) but by the recurrence of misfortune, our misfortune, that makes Stoic principles perennially relevant. There has never been a shortage of people who suffer; there has been a shortage only of ways to comfort them. Stoicism meets the shortfall by bending and shaping itself to the different crises that arise in different historical moments, from the murderous political intrigues of the classical world to the terrorist attacks of the new millennium.

Driven always by contemporary events, Stoicism naturally captures the tenor of the times. Like a battery fully charged, it is ever ready. In ancient Rome it provided the guiding ethical framework for morally upright public officials—here, we must remember Seneca—who were obliged to serve tyrants and despots. To those frightened by the religious wars that overtook Europe in the sixteenth century, Stoicism appeared as a welcome source of moral instruction and refuge from civil strife. When our lives today become turbulent and unpredictable, we might profitably turn to Stoicism because it will help us to withstand all that is turbulent and unpredictable. When we feel that too much of what we face day after day is beyond our control, we might well take heart in the Stoic teaching that happiness resides only in those things we *can* control: our thoughts, intentions, and outlooks. Stoicism does not stop bad things from happening (no philosophy could), but it helps us to cope when they do happen and to remember that we can still be happy when misfortune clouds our life

All You Need Is Virtue

Cicero summed up Stoic ethics in the (for him) paradoxical belief that virtue is all you need for happiness. If, in any situation, you are inclined to do the morally right thing (which is what virtue means), then you will be happy—always and automatically, no matter what befalls you, or what does not. Amid all the vicissitudes of life, only virtue will bring you lasting contentment.

As Cicero knew only too well, this proposition clashed with Aristotle's more commonsensical, more forgiving view that external goods (health, wealth, etc.) are required for happiness because they enable us to put our virtue into action. Without them, Aristotle said, virtue can't really get started. If your strength is sapped by illness or hunger, you simply won't have the energy, physical or mental, to focus on leading the good life. To insist, then, that virtue—which is an inward disposition—is sufficient for happiness is to insist that nothing in the external world can affect our happiness, neither augmenting nor diminishing it. The outside world leaves no mark on your happiness: such is the Stoic view.

But suppose that happiness *were* vulnerable to forces in the external world. The consequences would be depressing. If your happiness depended on favorable circumstances—random good luck—then you could never be sure of finding it, no matter how virtuous you were. Uncertain of the future, you could only, as Cicero put it, "pray heaven that happiness might somehow come our way."[2] And as you wait for Dame Fortune to locate you on her Global Positioning System, you would eventually conclude that there is no virtue to being virtuous. True, you might one day stumble upon happiness—it could be no more calculated than that—but it would not be virtue that made you stumble.

If happiness really does entail the possession of goods that depend partly on chance—health, wealth, fame, and success—then it would be a rarity in human history, for most people who have ever lived on this planet have not enjoyed the opportunities for upward mobility that you and I take as our birthright. Can this really be the sort of happiness that we want? Why should happiness be a locked door that might (or might not) spring open and let us slip through to the other side? Surely, the happiness we wish for is a happiness that, however difficult to achieve, does not disqualify anyone from trying. For the Stoics (and most likely for us, too) happiness must be open to everyone on equal terms, accessible to all in the circumstances of life as we live it here and now. Only then, because we have made the effort to obtain it, can we say that our happiness is not in jeopardy, but safe and secure. It is something we *own* and not just something we chance upon, like a shiny penny in the street.

To use a favored Stoic analogy, we can no more command events in the world than the sailor can alter the direction of the wind. But our happiness does not thereby suffer, because it does not depend on events in the world; it depends only on the "brilliance" of our virtue (as Cicero put it), a brilliance that no turn of worldly events can obscure or overwhelm.[3] No misfortune, no run of bad luck, will ever destroy or overthrow our happiness. No matter how much misery a happy man endures, he remains happy. The Stoic secret of happiness is that it lies in possessing only those things that fortune cannot steal from us, and those things always come down to good character.

Now that is an astounding proposition, and one that you might greet with skepticism, if not downright dismissal. Even the ancients felt unsure about it, for they debated the question endlessly. Imagine, as they did, a happy person—that is, a virtuous person—who is unjustly imprisoned and savagely beaten by his captors. A Stoic will argue that this person remains happy throughout his imprisonment, even at the very moment when the punches and blows fall upon him. Certainly he feels the agony of his torments and wishes them to stop, for he is only human; but no torment, however severe, can rob him of his happiness. As Cicero confidently declared, happiness "will not tremble, however much it is tortured."[4] That was exactly the attitude that Stockdale took toward his suffering in the prison camps of North Vietnam. Less invitingly, the Stoic principle works the other way around: no amount of good fortune will make you happy. If you're unhappy and then win the lottery, you stay unhappy: new riches, old miseries.

Perhaps you believe that things other than virtue are good, and thus likely to be sources of happiness: health, wealth, pleasure, honor, talent, beauty, and brains. If such properties really *are* good, then happiness can arise from any of them (or disappear if taken away) and need not depend solely on virtue. To counter that view, a Stoic would argue that such things are *not* good, at least not intrinsically so, because they can be used for either good or bad purposes; they can either help or harm. In fact, nearly everything we might assume to be morally good turns out to be morally *neutral*. Example: a rich man can use his wealth to be a philanthropist or to support terrorism. Each enterprise requires money, but the money itself is morally neutral. What matters is the intention, be it moral or immoral.

By the same token, supposedly bad things turn out to be morally neutral. Just as health and wealth are not inherently good, poverty and disease are not inherently bad. No reasonable person, a modern-day Stoic would claim, concludes that someone is immoral just because he or she cannot afford to pay the electricity bill. He or she might be ill, or unemployed, or barely able to feed and clothe his or her children. Our delinquent bill-payer could still be immoral, but it would have to be for reasons other than his or her failure to add to the profits of the utilities industry. Similarly, only a bigot—a person swayed by irrational fears—would denounce someone as immoral just for being HIV positive. If such a person were immoral it would, again, have to be for different reasons. Although hard-line politicians on both the left and the right do their best to convince us otherwise, to be poor or sick is no moral failure. Yet, as the wise Reb Tevye sardonically remarked in *Fiddler on the Roof,* it's no great honor, either.

Still, no rational person chooses to be destitute rather than solvent, ill rather than well. (It is precisely through such choices that we demonstrate our rationality.) Experience alone tells us that we do not, in fact, regard all morally neutral things as equally desirable: generally, we seek to enjoy health and wealth and to avoid sickness and poverty.

The Stoics made that same distinction. They rounded up all the supposedly good (but actually morally neutral) things in life and placed them in the special category of "preferred indifferents." Everything put in this category enhances our quality of life, and thus is preferred, but is not good in itself, and thus is morally indifferent. We like having preferred indifferents, and we are right to like them, because they smooth out life's rough edges. Many people in major cities have lived through the nightmare of getting to the airport on public transportation, fighting crowds of commuters while struggling to carry large heavy suitcases. How immeasurably more pleasant to take a taxicab (and to be able to afford it). The taxicab is one of modern life's great preferred indifferents, along with penicillin and personal trainers. Such things, although they do not make us virtuous, make us feel better, and if we are feeling better, we might find it a little bit easier to behave better. You are much less likely to lose your temper in a roomy, air-conditioned taxicab than in a crowded, stinking, and stiflingly hot commuter train.

The wise man, as Seneca understood, knows how to handle preferred indifferents: he neither seeks "Fortune's bounty" nor rejects it, nor mourns its loss.[5] (In writing that, Seneca was answering his critics, who had charged that he enjoyed unmerited wealth and power simply because he was in the Emperor Nero's good graces.) Similarly, the wise man tolerates illness and injury, yet all the while wishes that he were healthy—not for the sake of health alone, but for the sake of all the good and useful things a healthy person can accomplish. This is the chief merit of all preferred indifferents and the reason it is honorable to prefer them: they afford us more opportunity to act virtuously. So it is right and natural and wise (although not, strictly speaking, necessary) to seek wealth and health and strength. Indeed, the Stoics believed that it was better for a wise man than a fool to be wealthy, as the wise man would use his wealth to perform good deeds, whereas the fool would not know how.

Smile at the Raging Storm

Neither desiring nor despising morally neutral things, the Stoic takes in stride whatever comes his or her way, be it pleasure or pain, reward or punishment, glory or infamy. It is wisdom to remain steadfast and even-tempered in the face of changing, uncontrollable events. So when fortune smiles, do not delude yourself by believing that its blessings will last forever; when misfortunes arise, as inevitably they will, take heart in knowing that they, too, will run their course. You need not fear misfortune because misfortune is not evil. Come what may, you must look on good and bad times alike with the same firm dispassionate resolve, the same fearless bold indifference.

As Admiral Stockdale knew firsthand, the power to persevere comes from within the mind. Like a fortress unassailable, it can grant us everlasting refuge (so the Stoics claim) from pain and adversity—and from the equally hazardous temptations of glory and renown. The citadel of the mind is breached only by the force of reason, as Hamlet, in meditative mood, understood: "Nothing is good or ill but thinking makes it so." We cannot steer events in the outside world, or even always anticipate them; what we *can* do is accept them, whatever they turn out to be, with calm intelligent reason. Only then might we attain freedom in a world dominated by events unwelcome and unbiddable.

There is more than a touch of Stoicism in the Hindu and Buddhist principle of detachment from the fruits of our labors. In harmony with Eastern spiritual traditions, Stoicism does not ask you to renounce the world, but to be independent of it, to be immune to its charms and seductions no less than to its taunts and threats. You gain that independence, that freedom, by protecting yourself from circumstances that you are powerless to control. And that is why the ancient Stoics devised exercises of restraint and self-control to steel themselves against injury and loss.

Many of these exercises will seem to us strange and harsh. When angry, hold a mirror in front of your face and look in disgust on your distorted features: you will never want to be angry again. (Seneca liked that one.) A Stoic technique that hints at modern cognitive therapy is to relabel unpleasant experiences. If trapped in a crowd (again, that packed commuter train), just think of it as a party, and then your emotions will change along with your thoughts. Other exercises have a touch of the morbid. Epictetus instructed his pupils to dwell on the thought, as they kissed their wife and children, that their loved ones were mortal and one day would die. When that day came, they would be ready for it.

But do not suppose that the Stoic's detachment renders him heartless, for his emotions run as deeply as anyone's, his pleasures feel as intense, his pains are equally acute. Shakespeare, again, shows us the emotional complexity of the Stoic hero. When Macduff learns the devastating news that Macbeth's henchman has slaughtered his entire family, his comrade urges him to bear his grief like a man. The stalwart soldier retorts, wisely and humanely, that he must also "feel it like a man." Macduff honors (but does not indulge) his feelings by using them as a spur to virtuous action, for no sooner does grief come upon him than he moves to plot the downfall of the tyrannous Macbeth.

In the same way, the Stoic sage uses reason to keep his feelings in check, thus preventing any single-minded pursuit of pleasure or avoidance of pain. Indeed, as Seneca cautioned, some pleasures—"blind and heedless devotion to one's affairs," "wild elation deriving from trivial and childish causes," "the idleness and decadence of a sluggish mind"— were simply corrupt.[6] Here, the contrast with Epicurus, for whom pleasure was the *dernier mot* of happiness, could not be stronger. Impassive in the face of pleasure and pain alike, the Stoic relies on reason's trustworthy guidance.

Stoicism provides a firm basis not for solitude and renunciation (let

Epicurus stay in his garden) but for direct action in the world. Recognizing a duty to participate in civil society, the Stoic makes decisions without exclusive regard to self-interest. Detached, then, from his own immediate welfare, just as he is detached from his feelings, he fixes his attention on the wider social sphere. He is like an archer who aims at a distant target.

That the Stoic cares for his neighbor is no accident. Through our rational powers, we all possess, as Cicero observed, a divine spark. This commonality binds us each to the other, requiring that we treat everyone as decently as we would treat ourselves. In this way, a necessary part of anyone's happiness is a concern for others. And so the concept of private ethics is alien to Stoic thought. No fundamental difference exists between the contemplative and active lives because contemplation is how we prepare for action; it is the thinking behind the doing. Thus, when Seneca says that virtue will be found "in the temples, the forum, the senate-house, standing in defence of the city walls, dusty and sunburnt, with calloused hands," he is linking it explicitly with public life.[7]

Precisely because it values the active life, Stoicism has appealed throughout history to statesmen, public servants, and politicians. And because a core Stoic principle is that misfortune cannot diminish happiness, we can hardly be surprised that it has been the philosophy of choice for good people in an age of despots. In ancient Rome, Stoicism found a highly receptive audience in state officials obliged to do a tyrant's bidding. Tyranny, like all external forces, was to be looked on with detachment and indifference. It was—and is—the way of the world that some leaders will be virtuous, some villainous. Yet throughout it all, the public servant soldiers on. Not for nothing was the watchword of the Roman Stoics *vivere militare:* "to live is to be a soldier." Facing with equal composure both freedom and despotism, and sustained by the knowledge that no imperial edict, no dictatorial fiat, could overthrow his happiness, the Stoic stands unshaken by liberty's fall and tyranny's rise.

Intimate with Suffering

They knew how to suffer, the Roman Stoics. Especially those unfortunate enough to live close to the center of power. Stoicism provided Cicero and Seneca with the intellectual basis for their opposition to autocratic rule, and for Marcus Aurelius it illuminated the virtuous path to be followed by a philosopher-king. With a characteristic Roman pragmatism (one of this culture's lasting achievements was the aqueduct), all three wanted to know how Stoicism could be practiced. Did it lead to the good life? Could it comfort honest men forced to serve dishonest masters? The answers lie in the story of their lives.

The Champion of Liberty

When Cicero (106–43 B.C.), the great Roman statesman, thought about happiness, he did so in frank awareness of the suffering he endured in both his political and personal life. In 63 B.C. he was named consul, the highest public office in the Roman republic, the form of government to which, against all odds, he remained lastingly loyal. During his consulship Cicero learned that Cataline was plotting to overthrow the republic and set up a dictatorship. Such treachery could not be countenanced, and so he quickly arrested the conspirators and summarily sentenced them to death. Cicero temporarily saved the republic (although not even he could reverse the gradual slide into civil war), but at great personal cost: Julius Caesar, who sought to hasten the republic's downfall, was now his enemy. Caesar, in shrewd retaliation, accused Cicero of malfeasance when he ordered the conspirators to be executed without a trial. Cicero was convicted of the charge and briefly exiled as his punishment. On returning to Rome he resumed his political career, but never again would he hold high public office.

Matters worsened during the civil war (49–44 B.C.), when Cicero supported Pompey, whom Caesar eventually defeated. Having backed the losing candidate, so to speak, Cicero faced the stark truth that he had no political future whatsoever and no alternative but to retire to his country villa in Tusculum. Scarcely a year later, Caesar, now established as dictator, granted him a full pardon. Make no mistake: this was no invitation to return to public office, but simply a confirmation that the humbled and exiled Cicero no longer posed a threat. A tyrant runs no risk in pardoning the powerless.

Or maybe just a little risk. After Brutus assassinated Caesar, Cicero argued for the restoration of his beloved republic. That was very much the wrong case to plead, and Cicero paid for his liberal opinion with his life. The triumvirate that wielded temporary power immediately after Caesar's death—Mark Antony, Octavius (the future Caesar Augustus), and Lepidus—decreed that Cicero must be killed. And so he was. With him died the dream of the Roman republic.

In Cicero's many moments of despair, what he desperately needed was a principle to live by. He found it in Stoicism, which he modified to create a distinctively personal philosophy. Welcoming the solace provided by the Stoic values of indifference, detachment, and tranquility, Cicero drew strength in dark times from his belief that philosophy "takes away the load of empty troubles, sets us free from desires, [and] banishes fears."[8]

But philosophy was no retreat from life; it was politics by other means. Through reading, thinking, and writing, Cicero continued his public career even though barred from public office. In his essays, letters, and dialogues he expressed the same ideas, the same principles, and the same tough practical wisdom that had guided his decisions when he was an esteemed public servant. By so devoting himself to scholarship he embraced the Stoic belief that the contemplative life benefits society because it teaches us through reflection how best to act in the world. Like the fabled Stoic sage, Cicero rejected as irrational the view that thought and action were irreconcilable opposites: "After serious and long continued reflection as to how I might do good to as many people as possible, and thereby prevent any interruption of my service to the State, no better plan occurred to me than to conduct my fellow-citizens in the ways of the noblest learning."[9]

This is philosophy, "the ways of the noblest learning," expounded by someone with a passion for the activity and energy of life, a passion felt all the more keenly when suddenly checked by rude fate. Forced repeatedly into exile or house arrest, Cicero was naturally drawn to a philosophy that prized equanimity: the ability to treat all things in the same manner, even-handed and controlled. Sharing the Stoic conviction that happiness was independent of chance events and circumstances, Cicero believed that if you are "capable of regarding all the hazards and accidents of fortune and human life as endurable," then you will have "every reason" to find happiness.[10] He then wrote about himself, preferring not to disguise his torments, and declared that his own banishment was no hardship. For the Stoic, all suffering is bearable.

The Tyrant's Tutor

Now is the time to take a longer look at Seneca's remarkable search for happiness in the midst of misfortune. He was banished to Corsica in A.D. 41 after the Emperor Claudius's wife, that shameless hussy Messalina, falsely accused him of committing adultery with the emperor's niece, Julia Livilla. Seneca lived in miserable exile on that barren island for eight years. For the Romans, the pain of exile was worse than we can today imagine, as it meant a complete loss of identity; in exile, a civilized man found himself cast out into the wilderness, forced to keep company with barbarians. It would be as if he lived with wild animals.

Seneca's fortunes improved only when Claudius's next wife, the cunning Agrippina, sister to the defamed Julia Livilla, recalled him to Rome and appointed him tutor to her twelve-year-old son (from an earlier marriage), Lucius Domitius, the future emperor Nero. That moment sealed Seneca's fate and swept him up in the turbulent affairs of an affable and popular young prince who went unbelievably bad.

In A.D. 54, so the gossipy historian Suetonius tells us, Agrippina, impatient for her son to ascend to the imperial throne, killed Claudius by feeding him poisoned mushrooms. During the young Nero's tyrannical rule, Seneca became a leading statesman, enjoying unforeseen wealth, power, and fame. Yet this prominence, which contrasted so sharply with the shame and disgrace of his years in exile, was a poisoned chalice. For it came at the price of having to submit to the emperor's every wish. Seneca was still Nero's slave; he was just a slave with unsurpassed influence. A mere five years into his reign, Nero, who had pledged himself so often to the virtue of clemency, renounced any pretense of goodness when he forced Seneca to plot the assassination of Agrippina—the emperor's own mother. (When Seneca received this damnable order, did he recall Cicero's words of warning that nobody who values his freedom can serve a tyrant?)

Imagine the turmoil Seneca must have felt when commanded to be an accessory to murder. After all, the Dowager Empress Agrippina was his patron, the woman who had secured his return from exile, had given him back his life. But neither was she the flower of maternal virtue; she had killed her husband and was rumored to harbor incestuous desires for her son. Still, was this how Seneca would repay Agrippina's generosity, by conspiring to kill her? A further abomination awaited. Seneca was compelled to justify the murder before his fellow senators. In publicly excusing his own crimes, Seneca dishonored the state he had given his life to serve. And yet he showed no reluctance, no inclination to curb the emperor's violent instincts. Appalled by the brutality of imperial politics, and shamed by his complicity in them, Seneca retired three years later and vowed, bitterly, never to return to public life.

Yet even in retirement Seneca could not escape Nero's cruelty, and days that should have been peaceful were just as precarious and intrigue-filled as they had ever been. In A.D. 65, only a few years after withdrawing from politics, Seneca was ordered to kill himself—an order that he had no choice but to carry out—because Nero suspected him of participating in a rebellious plot led by Calpurnius Piso. The evidence was flimsy (a letter to Piso expressing friendly sentiments), but it was enough to send Seneca to his death, for Nero was hardly willing to let a possible adversary live, especially one who could expose all his dirty tricks.

Tacitus, never one to shy away from a shocker, dramatized Seneca's slow and painful death in his *Annals of Imperial Rome*. Because he regarded the suicide as an act of heroic defiance, the ancient historian modeled his account on the similarly courageous death of Socrates, as recorded in Plato's *Phaedo*. Like the Greek philosopher before him, Seneca faced death with neither fear nor sadness. To his friends, in whose cherished company he died, he bequeathed his only remaining possession: "the pattern of my life."[11] As the centurion bearing the death sentence stood by, their tears elicited from the doomed man not sympathy but a rebuke: What had become of their philosophy that should give them the strength to withstand misfortune? Had it now deserted them, when they most needed it? No one should be surprised by Nero's heartlessness, Seneca calmly explained, for a man who murders his own mother will not think twice before killing someone as insignificant as his teacher. It would be no more to him than swatting a fly.

In his last moments, Seneca begged his wife, Paulina, to set a fixed term to her grief and console herself with the memory of his good deeds. Unwilling to live without her husband, Paulina insisted that she be allowed to die with him. Seneca praised her action as nobler than his own because she had chosen to sacrifice her life, whereas he had no choice at all. Prepared to end their lives together, they cut open veins in their arms with a single stroke. Seneca, because of his infirmity, bled too slowly, and so he also severed the veins in his ankles and behind his knees. Wishing to spare his wife the gruesome sight of his mutilated body, he requested that she be removed to an adjoining chamber. Nero, fearful of making himself even more unpopular, ordered that Paulina's wounds be stanched and that she be kept alive; he would not grant her a martyr's glory.

The unsuspecting Seneca, now surrounded by his companions, drank a cup of poison. When that did not kill him, he immersed himself in a warm bath to accelerate the blood loss. (Rubens's painting of this moment is appropriately dignified, but gets every historical detail wrong, including the style of Seneca's beard and the size of his bathtub.) At last nearing death, he was carried into a steam room, where the vapors finally suffocated him. In accordance with the instructions he had dictated when at the height of his power, Seneca was cremated without pomp or ceremony.

Throughout his traumatically unbalanced life, Seneca endured fortune and misfortune, prominence and exile, reward and punishment; he was forced to kill others and, finally, to kill himself. If anyone had good cause to meditate on the vagaries of life, it was he. He put his thoughts into writing, producing ten treatises on ethics that have survived solely because in the eleventh century the monks of Monte Cassino (the very place where the young Aquinas studied) transcribed them from a lost Latin manuscript. These works include *De vita beata* ("On the Happy Life"); *De tranquillitate animi* ("On Peace of Mind"), whose very name affirms a Stoic virtue; the *Consolatio ad Helviam* ("The Consolation of Helvia"), a formal letter written to his widowed mother to lessen her grief during his Corsican exile; and *De clementia* ("On Mercy"). Was it crafty politics—or desperate hope—that led Seneca to dedicate "On Mercy" to the eighteen-year-old Nero, then still young enough to learn a lesson in morality?

Over the centuries, Seneca has attracted countless readers because he has revealed that the secret of happiness (or at least *a* secret) is the power of the rational mind to triumph over adversity. But there is more: the secret turns out to be common knowledge. For it was "nature's intention," he confidently explained, "that there should be no need of great equipment for a good life: every individual can make himself happy."[12] But Seneca also knew that some of his contemporaries (the Epicureans, most likely) dismissed Stoicism as a trick, or confidence game, which deceives us about the harsh realities of poverty, illness, and suffering. It was simply disingenuous, his critics claimed, to teach (as Seneca did) that suffering was not actually suffering if we refused to accept it as such. No matter how many fancy arguments we contrive, the poor man still faces his poverty, the sick man his illness, and the lonely man his despair.

But I think that so negative a view misses Stoicism's central point, which is not to mask or trivialize suffering—but to give us the means of *enduring* it. Yes, Stoicism speaks to our feelings of misery, discontent, and loneliness, but it speaks to them so that we need not be enslaved to them. If our happiness means anything, it means possessing, as Seneca put it, "a mind which is free, upright, fearless and unshakeable, untouched by fear or desire."[13]

The Philosopher-King

Seneca's problem was timing. He had the bad luck to live in an age of tyrants. Born a century later, he would not have endured the same misfortunes because he would have served the enlightened emperor Marcus Aurelius (121–180), another figure we have already met. Marcus spent much of his reign in battle, defending the empire from the barbarians across the Alps. He died, as they say, with his boots on, during a military campaign near Vienna. The emperor's personal life was marred by misfortune, including recurring illness, the loss of his father during his childhood, the premature death of most of his children, and rumors of his wife Faustina's infidelity. Yet the nearly two decades of his rule were idealized as a golden age: a time when philosophers really did become kings, and with wisdom governed the commonweal. The idealization began early, during the intensely unpopular rule of his son and successor, Commodus. The twelve-year reign of cruelty and corruption ended only with the assassination of the hated son of a heroic father.

As the philosopher-king incarnate, Marcus took seriously the responsibilities of government, to the point of sulking about it. Struggling to live in accordance with philosophical principles, he recorded his beliefs (and his confessions and his self-reproaches) in a private little book that we now call the *Meditations*. The book is not a formal treatise, a doctrinal statement, or even a loose collection of philosophical precepts. It is, rather, a moral diary: a gathering up of thoughts at the end of each day, however long, wearying, or bloody the day had been. The prose is brief and terse throughout, as if Marcus were writing in the margins of his time. Which, in view of his weighty political and military responsibilities, was certainly the case. Although his commitment to austere self-examination was hardly idiosyncratic (it was, in fact, the very method recommended by Epictetus, whose writings Marcus had carefully studied), it resulted in a deeply personal document of one man's struggle to live virtuously, and thus happily.

Stoicism appears in the *Meditations* not as an unattainable goal, but as a way of feeling at home in the world. Indeed, that is why it speaks to us today: because we, too, long to feel at home in the world. Like his contemporaries, Marcus was concerned less with the idealized vision of the Stoic sage (so ideal that no one could live up to it) than with the daily grind of being a good person. The Stoic unflinchingly surveys the trials and tribulations of his life, but always from the standpoint of a dogged confidence in the universe's fundamental coherence, rationality, and purpose. His constant conviction was that through sheer willpower he could move beyond unbridled desire to serene detachment. And so Marcus commanded himself to "wrestle" to become the sort of man that "Philosophy" wished him to be.[14] Happiness feels like wrestling not because it requires opponents to be defeated (in fact, there are no opponents because happiness lies within each person) but because it requires *us* to be ready and vigilant.

That the *Meditations* is one of the great bestsellers of Western philosophy is doubtless because Marcus was not a philosopher. But he was someone who wrote an intimate account of how philosophy could be a guide to right conduct. In keeping with the Stoic virtue of indifference, the *Meditations* is largely untroubled by contemporary events and incidents, a feature that also accounts for its timeless appeal. It was as if Marcus banished mundanities from his mind and raised the level of his attention to the larger questions of how life can be worthy and good. He pitched his thoughts perfectly: high enough to transcend everyday concerns, but not so high that he became (or we become) lost in abstractions. Marcus's words heal the worries and anxieties that beset not just himself eighteen centuries ago, but also the readers beyond number who have profited, and do profit, from his practical wisdom.

Sweat, Dirt, and Grease

Blaise Pascal, the seventeenth-century French philosopher and mathematician, declared, in a withering critique, that the Stoic knows the grandeur of mankind but not its humanity. Perhaps the French savant was thinking of Epictetus's brutally cynical remark that a new love affair is like a crystal wine glass: it's only a matter of time before it shatters. Beyond question, the Stoic code of behavior is harsh and austere; mere mortals find it nearly impossible to uphold such exacting standards of constancy. For those of us who have not yet climbed wisdom's steep and winding path, or have failed in the attempt, Stoic values will not necessarily make things easier for us.

Like some parent impossible to please, Stoicism refuses to accept that failure, too, plays a role in the drama of humanity, that failure is part of what makes us human. It refuses any acknowledgment that pain and suffering are not merely hardships to be endured but, more crucially, experiences that might teach us about life's nature and purpose. (The Book of Job, coming up in the next chapter, has one or two things to say on the matter.) Yes, the Stoic reaps the incontestable benefits of standing firm in adversity. Come what may, the Stoic endures, and endurance is a marvel to behold. But in between all that hardening and toughening we might lose sympathy for fellow travelers and become incapable of fathoming the depth of our own feelings. Tenacity, as Pascal understood, comes at a great price; a rock, for all its strength, is just a rock.

So here we must confront Stoicism's dark side: its contempt for the flesh-and-blood aspects of life. Such distaste for living in the world accounts for the uncomfortably morbid demeanor of many Stoic writers, and no one surpasses Marcus Aurelius for ruminating on the world's irreversible slide into decay and death: "Some things are hastening to be, others to have come and gone, and a part of what is coming into being is already extinct."[15] As Marcus knew, the passage of time brings ever closer the moment not of our dignity, but of our demise. To use the language of science, the world is governed by the law of entropy: everything runs down, moving into disorder, chaos, and eventual collapse.

Marcus's aversion to the natural shape of everyday life made for some disagreeable analogies. He exhorts himself to remember, in the very moment of sexual bliss, that his body is nothing but a carcass, whose destiny is to rot away. Forcing home the classic Stoic point that happiness does not depend on external things, he judges that "as your bath appears to your senses—soap, sweat, dirt, greasy water, all disgusting—so is every piece of life and every object." No doubt Marcus's bathwater was disgusting (especially after a day on the battlefield), but it takes a profound alienation from your own body to believe that the best image for life is dirt and grease and stink. Not surprisingly, Marcus retreats into the pristine fortress of his own mind, where he can put himself safely beyond the reach of bodily injury, worldly misfortune, and bathtub scum.[16]

Other people's bodies could be equally foul. Unlike his subjects, Marcus did not enjoy the gladiatorial combats performed in amphitheaters. (No doubt he preferred the real thing, where honor was to be gained on the true field of battle.) So distasteful did he find blood sports—he complained they made him nauseous—that he preferred during the contests to read his mail. The thousands of Romans gathered in the Coliseum for the excitement and brutality of the games could not have failed to witness Marcus's overt performance of Stoic indifference. No secret did the emperor make of his reluctance to witness the atrocities that passed for public entertainment; duty alone explained his presence. He ordered gladiators to fight with blunted points on their spears and dulled blades on their swords, much to the dismay of bloodthirsty audiences who, through their shouts and roars, demanded that any gladiator who had not put up a good fight be killed on the spot. The crowds may have been insulted that their emperor showed more interest in state documents than the well-matched combatants in the arena below, but Marcus remained implacable in the face of their displeasure. He did not require "the praise of the multitude" to make him happy.[17] No Stoic ever does.

8

THE HIDDEN FACE OF GOD
(JUDAISM)

About twenty-five hundred years ago (although not even the scholars can settle on the date) a Hebrew poet turned an old story about a Bedouin sheik into a paean to suffering so majestically powerful that still today we stand in awe of its radical wisdom. We do not know who wrote the Book of Job, or when or where. If there were several authors, their hands have left no trace. To say that the poet (or poets) lived in the ancient Near East, somewhere between the Persian Gulf and the shores of the Nile, does not much help the matter. For the story is set in the lost land of Uz, and it refers to none of the major events in the history of the Israelites: the call of Abraham, the Exodus from Egypt, or the captivity in Babylon. Nor can we be sure that Job himself is a Hebrew, for he says nothing about the kings of Israel or the prophets and their teachings. Yet he is no pagan: he contends with the one God, the creator of heaven and earth.

With no historical clues to guide us, we must see Job as a solitary figure, stripped of mere locality; he is beholden to no one creed, is attached to no single tribe, stands for no particular man. Or, rather, he stands for every man. In him we recognize the agonizing truth that suffering is a scar on every human life. For who among us has not felt what Job has felt and demanded as he demanded to know the answer to the riddle of suffering? Whoever the Job poet was, he was someone who had a conception of what suffering means: the pain, the misery, the lonely burdens, the unanswered sorrowful cries, and the senseless ruin of it all. He must have lived in a world where injustice ran free, trampling goodness under its heavy foot, and he would not be surprised to know that, sadly, our world is much the same.

In the days before misfortune shadowed his life, Job was pious and upright and feared his God. There was no cause for that God to punish his faithful servant, and yet he chose, almost on a whim, to do just that. The story begins as Satan, that mischief-maker of old, insinuates that Job is virtuous only because he is prosperous, that his faith would retreat at misery's first attack. God confidently accepts the wager and tests Job's loyalty—by ruining his life. First, his possessions are stolen. But that is nothing compared to what follows: his children are killed, crushed by the weight of the family home as it collapses in a tornado; then affliction strikes the man himself, when oozing sores and scaly lesions cover his skin. Tortured, Job sits in the smoldering embers of what had been his home and scratches his cankerous flesh with a pottery shard retrieved from the rubble.

In his abject misery he is visited by three friends: Eliphaz, Bildad, and Zophar. As a mark of respect for Job's suffering, they sit with him in silence for seven days. But when they do speak, these men are fiercely critical—these men who should have sustained their friend with sympathy and love. In ever more menacing tones, they tell Job that he suffers because he has been wicked (even if no one can say exactly how) and that God always punishes the wicked just as he always rewards the virtuous. This is old theology, a spouted piety: man reaps as he sows. If only Job would repent his sins, then his misery would cease. "But I have not sinned!" Job protests. He knows that he is a good man, and better than most. "I hold fast to my righteousness and will not let go.

My heart has not blasphemed all my days." Blameless to the last, he does not deserve the affliction that God has sent him. So why did God send it? The answer remains hidden.

Suddenly, a new character bursts onto the scene: Elihu, the angry young man—angry that Job thinks himself more righteous than God and angry that Eliphaz, Bildad, and Zophar have not answered Job's question. Though forceful in speech, this young hothead comes across no better than the venerable elders for whom he shows nothing but contempt. Not yet has Job been answered.

What makes Job such a modern (or is it timeless?) character is that he is a skeptical, restless, and even rebellious soul. Though he encounters the world as a place of waste and suffering, still he believes in the goodness and perfection of his God. Cursed though he is by hard injustice, he does not dismiss life as meaningless but hungrily searches for its meaning. When he cannot find it, he demands—and yet how poorly that word conveys Job's fist-shaking impatience—that God reveal the meaning to him. Never does Job contemplate suicide, for he seeks not escape from life, but life's fulfillment. Others might succumb to despair, and quickly so, but Job insists that life is always and unconditionally meaningful, even in the wretched here and the awful now. Here on the dung heap and now in the moment of misery.

Such is Job's sublimely human stance. The world is good because a good God created it. And it is in human existence that the creator's goodness is most plentifully manifest, for we *can* question him—and he *will* answer us. There is no reason, then, for goodness to be absent from our life at any moment. Job does not want, nor does he expect, to postpone the satisfactions of life until the promised afterlife. True, he mourns his loss—"My flesh is clad in worms and dust"—for he is only human, but he believes throughout that joy and goodness will also come his way: "I hoped for good, but evil came./I looked for light, but gloom came." Job's steadfastness—to look for light in the midst of gloom—tells us that it is not right that we should find only evil and be covered only in darkness. God did not create this world for us to despise it and to long for release from its vale of tears. The world exists, rather, that we might find some fulfillment in it (even if our faith tells us that the greatest fulfillment lies in the hereafter). As surely as we are called to endure suffering in this life, we are invited to enjoy happiness. And in a way that seems hardly possible, scarcely acceptable, suffering is what readies us for happiness.

Emboldened by righteousness, Job decides that God must be put on trial and held accountable for the suffering that with wanton cruelty he has inflicted on an innocent humanity. God is the maker of man, but also man's downfall and his ruin, Job charges. "Your hands shaped me and fashioned me/Only to destroy me totally." Audaciously, he will prosecute the case himself, for he demands nothing less than the right to challenge God to his face: "I would press my suit to his face." God, in turn, must show evidence of Job's guilt or admit that he is blameless and has suffered without cause—in which case, God himself is guilty of a horrible injustice. Call it bravery, call it bluster, but it is no modest wish to put God in the witness stand. Yet it is Job's wish, and he does not shrink from it.

God, however, does seem to shrink from it, for he is nowhere to be found. "Why do you hide your face?" Job beseeches. The divine suspect, who is also the divine judge, is on the run, a fugitive from himself:

> Behold, if I go east—he is not there;
> West—I do not discern him;
> North—in his concealment I cannot behold him;
> South—he is hidden and I cannot see him.

There is something beyond mere accusation in Job's words, for they are taunting. God must face the facts, or the facts will condemn him, condemn him as the weak God who cannot overthrow evil, or the cruel God who will not. As long as God hides his face, the problem of suffering cannot be solved. Job finally forces a confrontation with his mysterious persecutor. In defiant mood, he *will* have his answer.

Out of the whirlwind, it comes. At last God raises his voice, shows his face, and gives his answer. But he gives it on *his* terms, not Job's. He does not answer the complaint—the wager with Satan and the shocking injustice done to Job are simply forgotten—but rather challenges the challenger. (The evasion is not for lack of words: this is God's longest speech in the Hebrew Bible.) In an abrupt reversal, it is man who stands trial for doubting God's governance of the world. It is the questioner who now must search out the answer. With the sting of a lash comes the humiliating charge, "Where were *you* when I laid the earth's foundations?" The force of it flattens Job, who confesses, "Behold I am small; how can I refute you?"

Yet Job is not completely vanquished, for he admits only his ignorance, the ignorance that he shares with every other child of Adam. Though he has been chastised for presuming to know more than his maker—how can the creature judge the creator?—he has not been branded a sinner. Despite the presumption of Job's so-called friends, there is no sin to brand him. And so, in the story's epilogue, God restores—nay, multiplies—Job's fortunes, sending him twice the number of sons lost and daughters more beautiful than before. He lives on happily for another 140 years, more blessed than he ever imagined he might be.

The wheel turns one last time, only Job does not know it. God remembers his faithful servant's moral courage and praises him for having "spoken the truth." And that is why God sides with Job: because he alone found the strength to contend with God, to wrestle with life's perplexities and penetrate its secrets. Job does not know that the wheel has turned, but we do. We know the last triumphant truth of his bitter agony: that it is right to demand more and better from the world, right to seek meaning in life as it comes to us, and right to expect happiness in the midst of unspeakable suffering.

In the story of Job we find an almost cosmic definition of happiness, one more abstract than we have seen and one far removed from any simplistic notion that happiness has anything to do with pleasure or good fortune. Through this parable of suffering we see happiness in an unaccustomed but penetratingly clear light—as bound up in our search for the meaning of life when life seems most meaningless. In some sense, happiness *is* the search for meaning against all odds. Which is why suffering is no barrier to happiness but a means—so improbable, so unwelcome—for discovering just what happiness is.

Freely Imperfect

The Talmud, the rabbinical commentary on the Hebrew Bible that has been developed and studied over centuries, speaks of God's humility in creation. God deliberately curtailed his powers and allowed himself to call into being the poor imperfect substance that is us. Our imperfections—causing harm, doing wrong, making others suffer—mark us out as God's fallible creatures. When he could have done otherwise, God limited his unbounded goodness to create within us the possibility of evil. Our most damning flaw is the surest sign of our humanity. Animals are ferocious but not evil; nor do the angels risk villainy. Only we sin.

But as the rabbis caution, we should not cultivate that flaw. The rosebush bears thorns, but that does not mean we should prick ourselves on them. Better that we do not. Evil exists in somewhat the same way: so that we might avoid it. If evil possesses a value, it is never a face value, but only a submerged one. We cannot find any forthright merit in something so senseless, so irrational as evil. And yet we might find merit half-hidden. If we must credit evil, then let us credit it as the price to be paid for knowing—and doing—what is right and what is good.

In *Faith after the Holocaust* (1973), the Jewish philosopher Eliezer Berkovits (1908–1992) maintains that without evil there can be no good, for each presupposes the other in the way that contrary things always do. Just as we know light as the opposite of darkness, or heat as the opposite of cold, we know good as evil's opposite. If vice were not a possibility, then virtue would not be an actuality, for what is virtue but the conscious rejection of vice? Evil exists that we may spurn it, and in that spurning know ourselves as inherently moral beings, as beings capable of creating happiness in our lives by filling it with virtue.

But virtue, as Berkovits reminds us, must be freely chosen, because our choosing is what matters. To be virtuous under compulsion—you would like to shoplift, but you don't because the closed-circuit television camera would expose you—is to be not virtuous, but only obedient. Virtue arises only when you *could* do something wrong and then do not. Our freedom to choose good over evil depends, Berkovits insists, on our own imperfection. Only imperfect things can change, and for that very reason only they are free.

Though it seems incredible, our freedom rests on our failure. For it is only when the gap is exposed between the world as it is and as it might be that we are spurred on to make decisions and take action. You and I are not entirely good, but we can become better—or worse. And so the hope for our improvement is also the threat of our decay, for at any moment, depending on our actions, humanity can either climb upward or spiral down. Such is the awesome responsibility of our freedom.

God's Unspeakable Silence

The question of suffering arouses fiery passions and enraged accusations against God. The question is never answered, but the passions are cooled and the questioner finds at last some peace. Job's peace was not that God answered him (he did not) but that God was *present* to him. "I have heard of you with my ears/But now my eyes see you." And that was enough for Job, who, despite the troubles and trials heaped upon him, never faltered in his faith. If Job had renounced his faith, he would not have bothered with God, because to him God would be dead. Despite the understandably angry urgings of his wife, Job did not abandon his God, even though it seemed that his God had abandoned him.

Job insisted that God conform to Job's own expectations and bend his divine shape to a merely human will. Our mistake, too, is to presume that God will manifest himself in human history in just the way we want him to. Proudly, we demand a God of our own devising, one who is forever ready to protect his faithful servants and subdue their enemies. But history mocks our expectation that God should work to our schedule and not his own. The Holocaust, genocide in Rwanda, the attack on the World Trade Center—these are but a few examples of thousands that could be named—tell us that God presents himself in history mostly as the uninvolved bystander, the silent witness to abomination. God is silent, too, in the intimate history of our lives, in prayers that he does not answer and midnight terrors he does not banish.

But why is God silent? If he wished, he could intervene in history at any moment to punish the guilty. But that would turn the world into a kind of prison, for we would live in constant fear of punishment. Like a puppet that moves only on command, we would obey God only under coercion, and thus perform an illusion of freedom. But we were not created to be puppets, and it is ludicrous to speak of a puppet's happiness. We were created to be free and to use our freedom to forge our happiness.

It is to safeguard our necessary freedom, the Jewish philosophers have taught, that God shows his presence in history more by restraint than strength. Like a parent who shows forbearance to a misbehaving child, God displays through his inaction a strength beyond brute force. He willingly casts himself into shackles and renders himself powerless in the face of evil so that our dignity can be preserved and our freedom guaranteed. In Berkovits's arresting metaphor, God cannot "bludgeon" us into goodness.[1] So instead of asking Why is God silent? let us ask What happens to us in God's silence? One answer is that he preserves the possibility of our creating meaning and purpose in the world even in its most despairing moments, and so gives us the chance of working toward happiness. Not a happiness that entails pleasure or the satisfaction of desire, but one that makes us authentically alive, more real than we have ever been.

Why sleepest thou, O Lord?

Although it resonates deeply for the generations that struggle to keep their faith after Auschwitz, the Talmudic doctrine of *hester panim,* "the hiding of the face," dates from biblical times. We remember (and perhaps echo, too) Job's mournful cry of divine injustice, "Why do you hide your face?" The prophet Isaiah calls God El Mistater, the hidden God: "Verily thou art a God that hidest thyself, God of Israel, Savior." It is crucial, though, that for Isaiah the hidden God is a *saving* God, not a cruel one. The psalmist, too, wrote of that grievous moment when God, made sorrowful by the cruelty of his creation, looked the other way:

Awake, why sleepest thou, O Lord?
Arise, cast us not off for ever.
Wherefore hidest thou thy face,
And forgettest our affliction and our oppression?
For our soul is bowed down to the dust:
Our belly cleaveth unto the earth.
Arise for our help,
And redeem us for thy mercies' sake.[2]

How in that silence can we ever hear his voice? What the rabbis propose stretches all credulity: that God's silence is the symbol not of his absence—but of his *presence*. Like a child playing hide-and-seek (to venture an impertinent simile), God is still present, but out of sight and waiting to be found. Although we are unaware of him, he is still *there*, in the game, like the child crouched underneath the table or lurking behind the chair. Of course, the analogy quickly finds its limit, for we do not experience God's absence in anything like a playful spirit. It comes upon us, rather, as the distress of abandonment and the torture of doubt. We look and look for a sign of the creator's loving presence, and from here to the horizon's far edge we find nothing at all.

Why does God hide? Not because we force him, for we cannot compel the almighty. God's indifference is not a disapproving judgment on us, not a punishment or sign of his anger. It is, rather, part of his divine nature: he is the God who hides. And he hides for a reason that we have come upon again and again: our freedom. To be good you must choose to be so; but to choose, you must be free. Through the gift of freedom, God gives us scope to be human. Although he hopes that we use the gift wisely, he knows that we might not. And so he waits. As God waits for goodness to shine through, the world descends into evil. The wicked prosper and the violent conquer and the oppressors triumph. There is no alternative, and there is no cause to regret it. For us to be human we must be free to choose evil; for God to be God he must grant the choice.

Such is the moral contradiction of our world. God denies his essence, allowing the world to be imperfect when he could have made it perfect and scarcely noticed the trouble he had taken. So that goodness may triumph—if not today, then a joyful someday—he permits the scourge of evil. When evil does rise up in the world, God hides his face as the sign that he accepts such a baleful necessity. As the Psalms so movingly express, the paradox of divine existence is that God, to show his love, abandons some of us to a fate so heartless that we experience it as brutal indifference to our blameless suffering. We suffer not because we are guilty, but because suffering is our common lot. Job is entitled to be angry at his misfortune, but he is not entitled to be angry with his God, for God is not misfortune's cause.

In our life we may come to know what Job knew: that the problem of evil can *never* be answered in a way that will satisfy us. We cannot make sense of bad things for there is nothing comprehensible about them. Not everything happens for a good reason, although we wish that were true—and so often we are told it *is* true—because at least that would give us comfort when comfort is most needed. But the hard truth is that the wound of suffering pains us deeply, no matter how cleverly we theorize our dilemma, no matter how artfully we try to explain it away. In the face of our distress, God is silent: the voice that spoke to Job out of the whirlwind did not answer the charge of injustice, did not even admit that injustice had been done. But with an insistence that rivals Job's, we may ask not why God is silent, but what happens in that silence. And like Job, we shall be answered.

Our answer comes in the voice of tradition, a voice telling us that the mystery of God's silence is explained by the change that it brings about in *us*. That, too, is what Job discovered: we are changed—and possibly for the better, though of that there can be no guarantee—by circumstances not of our approval, let alone our design. We cannot expect that suffering's harshness will fade away, for its causes (mere accident, malicious intent) will always be found in our world. Yet we can expect, or at least hope, that suffering will bring about a change within us. In the ruins of suffering, in the blank unreasonableness of it all, we can strive to build up a meaning to life and thus cling to happiness. Never because of suffering but only in its spite, for always we wish that the opportunity had never come along. Like the desert patriarch in the ancient lost land of Uz, we can choose to be worthy of our trials and our torments, finding a meaning to life in the midst of our suffering, a meaning that no punishing darkness can ever extinguish.

Worthy of Our Suffering

This is no empty proverb, detached from worldly concerns or untested in the crucible of hard experience. It is a perennial truth ever to be discovered anew, and so it was found again in the grim time of the Holocaust. The systematic annihilation of European Jewry in the Nazi death camps stands as a perverse monument to pure evil. As such, it has raised questions not only about Judaism itself, but about the future of humanity. The horror of the Holocaust has made us realize that our Age of Reason has not put an end to barbarism. But it has also made us realize that within us survives the need for fulfillment beyond expectation. Sixty years on, the Holocaust demands that we continue to resist evil—by having hope for the world.

In his classic memoir *Man's Search for Meaning,* the famed Viennese psychotherapist Viktor Frankl (1905–1997), himself a survivor of Auschwitz, wrote that in any circumstance, no matter how dire, we retain our spiritual freedom: an independence of mind and soul, even when the body is bound and fettered by uncontrollable forces. "We who lived in the concentration camps," Frankl recalled, "can remember the men who walked through the huts comforting others, giving away their last piece of bread. They may have been few in number, but they offer sufficient proof that everything can be taken from a man but one thing: the last of the human freedoms—to choose one's attitude in any given set of circumstances, to choose one's own way."[3]

These are inspiring words (and ones that call to mind the heroism of Seneca, Cicero, and all the other Roman Stoics) for they help us to see how suffering can be a proud achievement. Not, to be sure, one that we seek out—there is no merit in needless suffering, let us continue to be clear about that—but one that steals upon us in the course of life. In desolate circumstances, when we are denied all possibility of positive action, when we can change nothing—nothing except ourselves—our sole achievement may be to endure our sufferings honorably. *How* you accept an unavoidable fate, *how* you shoulder your burdens, is what makes all the difference. The decision to endure is freedom's last stand: the final chance, as Dostoevsky would put it, to be "worthy of your suffering."

What a noble sentiment! But perhaps fraudulent, too. What does it mean to suffer worthily? It means, first of all, a stubborn refusal to be defined and determined by circumstance alone. We are not hostages to fortune, though fortune (be it good or bad) will have its due. Rarely can we decide what will happen to us, but always we decide what will *become of us.* That is so, Frankl explains, because the sort of person we wish to become rests on an "inner decision," one that need not be forfeited in the face of adversity.[4] As the deaths of the martyrs in the concentration camps testify, there is a hallowed dignity even in life's final wretched moments. Despair is the wrong conclusion to be drawn from the unalterable fact of suffering, for that is to concede that our response is likewise unalterable.

Yet there is a still higher meaning to the worthiness of suffering than moral courage. Our inner convictions—our anchor in a sea of troubles—must arise from somewhere. And that somewhere is the uniquely human recognition that, as Frankl puts it, we live *sub specie aeternitatis,* under the aspect of the eternal. Our life is never entirely what it seems to be right now (and thus never fully perceptible at any one instant) because life is always provisional, always unfolding in the light of larger, ultimate concerns. It is part of our nature to understand that the source of our inner strength is embracing a future goal, be it a particular action, a certain kind of relationship, or a distinctive experience.

We must have a future to live *for,* and so we always live partly in anticipation—which, of course, can be either hopeful or despairing. Being fully human is never about brute animalistic survival, but always about living for something, or someone, other than ourselves. Life's fulfillment lies in our attachment to what transcends immediate experience and what rises above the petty concerns of today, however overwhelming they are or misleadingly urgent they seem. Which is why, as Frankl explains, we willingly put on the yoke of suffering—but only on the condition that our suffering has a meaning. Or rather, that it lets us forge a meaning. Our suffering is not punishment for our sins, not a lesson in humility, not a test of endurance, and not a mystery beyond comprehension. Suffering, in all its irrationality, all its senselessness, is life's call to us: the call to reexamine our false ideas about happiness, the call to witness the truth of our being.

Though he arrives at his conclusion in a specifically Jewish context, Frankl makes what he believes to be a general point. Indeed, he claims that the drive to find meaning—the "will to meaning," as he terms it—motivates every human life. The drive expresses itself, and healthily so, as a tension: the painful recognition of the gap between your life as it is and as it might be. Mistakenly, we presume that the blessed life is the carefree one, when no pressures bear down on us and no challenges rudely rise up. Such is the near catatonic state promoted by the modern pharmaceutical industry as the lifestyle of choice. But a life so static can scarcely be called human, for it lacks the propulsion of *futurity* that only humans possess: the galvanizing awareness that we live not just for today but for a tomorrow that we strive to make better. To worry that your life is not yet good enough is to be in a very healthy state of mind— one conducive to moral growth—even though in the moment you feel only distress. You are longing to be answerable for your own life, longing to be worthy of life itself. And thus deserving of some happiness.

Here again, we remember Job, who thought that the solution to the riddle of life's meaning was to accuse God of injustice. Yet what happened was that life's meaning was thrown back on him with a nearly crushing force, and he understood that the universe was not answerable to him, but he to it. "*I* will ask questions and *you* will inform me," Yahweh commanded in a voice that carries on the wind across the millennia. Although it would be marvelous indeed if we could learn the lesson some easier and gentler way (usually, we learn it through suffering), life is mostly about the questions that it asks of us, the demands it places on us, and the worthiness of our response to its commanding call. What does life expect of me? *That* is the question to ask yourself in the moment of suffering.

Happiness is what happens as you search for meaning in circumstances of such bewilderment and perplexity that they appear to render meaning absurd. Happiness is less the meaning itself than your quest for it, the conscious orientation of your life toward a future goal and a fuller purpose. So we might say that we do not create meaning in life so much as discover it. The meaning is there all the time, implicit, undeclared, and waiting patiently until we are ready to listen. But we find it hard to listen because we would rather be doing the speaking. We would rather be God than Job. So hard is it for us to listen that sometimes it takes the shock and roar of a whirlwind to silence us.

The Fire Within

If there is meaning in the totality of life, there is meaning in suffering, for it is as much a part of life's charted course as birth and death. Neither invited nor welcome, and to be avoided whenever possible, suffering is, nonetheless, part of what makes a life full and complete. To live as if suffering were an affront to our humanity and a barrier to our happiness is to miss the point of what it means to be human and happy.

In *With God in Hell,* his account of heroism and enduring faith in the Jewish ghettos and death camps, Berkovits recounts an incredible story of happiness in the face of suffering. A group of young Hasidic men imprisoned at Plaszow, a concentration camp just outside Krakow, were forced to jump into a pit that would become their mass grave. They knew that German soldiers would fire on them as they fell, so that if suffocation did not kill them, the machine guns would. "As if a fire had been lit within them," the Hasidim began "to sing and dance."[5] Oblivious to the armed soldiers, the young men danced their way to death as the spray of bullets hit their twisting bodies in midair. They imposed another rhythm, as it were, on their suffering; they remade their reality by forcing a supernatural order on the chaos of earthly experience. Through rebellion, they denied another, seemingly more powerful reality.

Berkovits believed (although he was not there) that in their final moments the innocent victims "lived their lives as Jews with an intensity and meaningfulness never before experienced."[6] Should we be shocked that he called this tragic episode a moment of supreme happiness? Is that not a gross moral imposture, turning something intrinsically evil into an unwitting good? Yet the moment's profound authenticity depended on the soldiers who did not hesitate to open fire; it could not have been otherwise. Those young men sanctified their lives in life's last moment, creating holiness in the midst of abomination. They found a happiness that delivered them from fear and did not forsake them in their hour of greatest peril. Scandalously, the price of their happiness was the reality of evil.

The reality of evil and the fact of suffering are the price of everyone's happiness. This is the lesson of the Holocaust and the lesson of the Book of Job: to live the kind of life you choose in the face of circumstances *never* of your choosing. And yet, is there really an alternative? The essence of one's being does not wait for a more congenial setting, a more propitious moment, a better time.

CONCLUSION

Because so much of our time in this book has been spent simply trying to understand the scope and scale of happiness, it would be negligent, in this concluding moment, not to shift our attention from the *seeking* to the *finding*. Without in any way pretending to offer the last word on the matter, I'd like to end by describing, all too briefly, what it might mean for us to find happiness. Of course, to put it that way is to overstate the case, to make it more of a departure than it actually is, for in truth we have been anticipating this moment all along. The insights (not mine; I am but conveying them) expressed in these final pages have been gradually gathering force. If the lives of Epicurus, Seneca, and Ghazali, the stories of Buddha and Prince Arjuna, and the mystery of Job tell us anything, they tell us that the seeking of happiness flows into the finding of it, just as the rushing waters of a river pour out effortlessly into the calm ocean depth, and so cease to rush.

The Relief of Being Ordinary

For me, the most liberating insight about the pursuit of happiness, liberating because it helps us to overcome so many threatening anxieties, is that we do not have to become someone else to be happy. In a way, this truth is trivial: How can we be other than who we are? But what is far from trivial is the disturbing and all too prevalent belief that to find happiness we must turn our backs on all that is familiar, forge a new life, journey to distant lands, perform extraordinary acts, exchange a dismal present for a fantastic future, or wish upon an auspicious star. Such efforts are wasteful because they squander the opportunity that is always before us: to become not someone else—that is the perverted goal of the "makeover" ethos—but a better version of the person we already are. Whoever we are, and in whatever circumstances we face—and for nearly all of us, they will be common and ordinary ones—the possibility of happiness surrounds us. We are always in the right place, though we do our best to forget it.

So let us cultivate a happiness that is authentically ours and let us be happy with the things that will make us so. To be authentically happy means to take possession of ourselves, to bring about the person we are in potential, to become *more real*. As Voltaire famously put it, "We must make our garden grow."

Action is the heart of an authentically happy existence because only in action do we attain fulfillment. Of course, action is not just striking out in the world, but a directed realization of the kind of person you imagine yourself to be. In that way, you give your life a coherent shape and rescue yourself from dissolution and waste. Through purposeful action, you *become* your future and in it find your contentment. You accomplish yourself. Is it too much, too paradoxical, to say that being happy feels like growing up? For we make our happiness as best we can within life as it comes to us, and do not find our happiness in some magical elsewhere.

The Homecoming of Happiness

To search for happiness is not to embark on a voyage to a distant exotic land, but to return home. Whether actual or symbolic, the homecoming is a common feature in many different stories about the quest for happiness. Though each is distinctive, all the stories reveal the general truth—the truth for all of us, no matter who, no matter where—that happiness must feel like something that we once knew, perhaps only dimly, but now are finding again, although this time with a greater resolve and a surer purpose. In a way, we are discovering a part of ourselves that we had never known.

Though self-help gurus, life coaches, and other purveyors of self-esteem might tell us otherwise, becoming happy is not a kind of deliberate consumer choice. We do not appraise paths to happiness dispassionately, as if we were on the lookout for a bargain, ready to negotiate the best deal we can. In a way, the path finds *us,* for it must always fit the shape and size of life as we live it right here and right now. We end up with the only kind of happiness that we can: one that suits us, that feels right for us because it is in sync with our life's rhythm and pace.

Within the Span of Our Days

It is a cliché that the secret of happiness must come to us like a bolt out of the blue. It is also wrong. The secret must be an open one, otherwise it would defeat its very purpose, which is that we should know it. We are born to be happy, for happiness is the perfection of our existence. And we *can* achieve it. Not easily, and perhaps not on our own. And maybe there is yet more happiness in the life to come. But somehow, against all odds and despite the trial of our suffering, we forge a happiness in this life.

Only an evil genius would create us to be happy and then make the achieving of it so damnably hard that we give up in torment and despair. Happiness cannot take us entirely by surprise, cannot steal upon us, because it is an enterprise that requires our investment. For all its connotations of blissful epiphany, happiness is a rather pragmatic affair. It must lie within our reach and fall within the span of our days.

Happiness for All

That we shall find happiness cannot be guaranteed. Which is another way of saying that, however much the desire industry tries to persuade us otherwise, we are not entitled to be happy. We are entitled only to work for it. This entitlement we *all* share, simply because we are human. The chance for happiness is an irreducible part of our being, a part from which no one can be disqualified.

Yet, for the pursuit of happiness to remain free and open, it cannot be contingent on the acquisition of esoteric knowledge or the profession of certain beliefs. When the right to find happiness comes with conditions—Yes, you can be happy, but only if . . .—it ceases to be a right; it becomes, instead, a privilege. And like all privileges, its conferral (and repeal) depends on someone else's authority. But we have only to be born to possess the right to make ourselves happy. It is a perversion of that right, and an offense against human dignity, to attach too many strings to the offer of happiness. So what matters is not that your pursuit of happiness is sanctioned by an authority figure (be it religious or secular) but that it works for you—that it actually makes you happy.

Bound to the World—and Beyond

We cannot find happiness in isolation. A certain amount of quiet and calm reflection is surely necessary just to understand what happiness means, but the activity of *becoming happy* is one that binds us to the world. Finding happiness means not despising the world but wanting to create a better one. We might say, then, that our happiness is nested in the world, for the world is where, over a lifetime, we patiently build up the layers of a habitat—and the action of habit is crucial here—that we can proudly call good.

Yet a happy life is also one of ideals, of symbols of something higher, greater, deeper, and vaster than ourselves. It is a profoundly human need to aspire to something *more* and to be carried by that aspiration beyond horizon's edge. We want to envision something that surpasses our selfish desires, that outstrips merely personal goals, and then we want to attain it. Of course, from time to time we shall fail in that attainment, but we shall have learned enough to know that we are stronger than our failures. Our life is an ever striving, and we call the striving happiness.

ACKNOWLEDGMENTS

When I told my friends that I was going to write a book on happiness, I was expecting them to be supportive. After all, friends are supposed to support each other. Plus, everybody's interested in being happy, right? I was not, however, expecting them to tell me how to write the book. Yet in varying degrees, that is exactly what they did. Although I have not followed to the letter all of their instructions, I have been humbled by their generosity. With gratitude and affection I acknowledge the advice and support of John Brodholt, Cynthia Burns, James Davies, Ellen Gainor, James Greenfield, Tom Hammack, Jim Holman, Steve Holman, Sonja Kuftinec, Ari Lipman, Joe Lordi, George Marcotte, Kirk Melnikoff, Stephen Orgel, Bill Patterson, Jeff Renzulli, Adam Trexler, Jack Wieland, and Aleksandra Wolska.

Alan Stewart, a superb scholar who has also written for a wide readership, provided sound practical advice. Tony Morris, despite being an editor at another publishing house, was endlessly encouraging and offered insightful comments on portions of the manuscript. Andrew Leek listened patiently over many months as I recounted each advance—and each setback—in the long march from proposal to publication. Matt Richardson, a terrific writer, offered much needed help at a critical juncture. From the beginning, Richard Cellini's advice has been indispensable. No one could ask for a more astute reader or a better friend.

Queen Mary, University of London, where I teach in the School of English and Drama, has been unusually supportive of this work. I thank Philip Ogden and Morag Shiach for granting me research leave to complete this book and for encouraging me to write for a wider audience.

To my friend and agent Peter Robinson, sufficient thanks can hardly be given here, or anywhere. It is scarcely adequate to say that this book could not have been written without his patient guidance and anchored confidence. Kim Witherspoon and David Forrer at Inkwell Management have my warmest thanks for handling the American publication of this book with unmatched dedication and professionalism. Colin Harrison has been a model editor, and I remain grateful for his unflagging enthusiasm for this project and his sensitive and thorough reading of the manuscript. Also at Scribner, Karen Thompson has most capably and cheerfully managed the day-to-day production process, and Judith Hoover copyedited the text with supreme skill and precision. To everyone at Scribner, my heartfelt thanks.

To this book's dedicatee belongs more honor than a mere dedication can bestow.

NOTES

Introduction

1. Richard Layard, *Happiness: Lessons from a New Science* (London: Allen Lane, 2005), p. 12.
2. Epicurus, *Letter to Menoeceus,* in *The Epicurus Reader: Selected Writings and Testiminia,* trans. and ed. Brad Inwood and L. P. Gerson, (Cambridge, MA: Hackett, 1994), p. 82.
3. Seneca, *De vita beata* 8, in *Seneca: Four Dialogues,* ed. C. D. N. Costa (Warminster, UK: Aris & Phillips, 1994).
4. Seneca, *Consolatio ad Helviam* 5, in *Seneca: Four Dialogues.*
5. Robert Nozick, *The Examined Life: Philosophical Meditations* (New York: Simon & Schuster, 1989), pp. 99–117.
6. J. M. Keynes, "Economic Possibilities for Our Grandchildren," in *The Collected Writings of John Maynard Keynes* (London: Macmillan, 1972), 9: 328.
7. *The "Meditations" of Marcus Aurelius Antoninus . . . ,* ed. R. B. Rutherford, trans. A. S. L. Farquaharson and R. B. Rutherford (Oxford: Oxford University Press, 1989), 6.30.

1. The Greatest Happiness (The Utilitarians)

1. Jeremy Bentham, *An Introduction to the Principles of Morals and Legislation,* 1791, ed. J. H. Burns and H. L. A. Hart (Oxford: Oxford University Press, 1996), p. 4.
2. Bentham, *Introduction,* 1.3, p. 12.
3. Bentham, *Introduction,* p. 12.
4. Bentham, *Introduction,* p. 11.
5. Bentham, *Introduction,* section 4 note, p. 38.
6. Bentham, *Introduction,* 17.8, p. 285.
7. Bentham, *Introduction,* 1.1, p. 74.

8. Quoted in V. J. McGill, *The Idea of Happiness* (New York: Frederick A. Praeger, 1967), p. 119.

9. J. S. Mill, *Autobiography of John Stuart Mill* (New York: Columbia University Press, 1924), p. 58.

10. Mill, *Autobiography,* p. 47.

11. Mill, *Autobiography,* p. 94.

12. Mill, *Autobiography,* p. 99.

13. Mill, *Autobiography,* p. 104.

14. Mill, *Autobiography,* p. 100.

15. Mill, *Autobiography,* pp. 110, 113.

16. *Collected Works of John Stuart Mill.* 33 vols., ed. J. M. Robson et al. (Toronto: University of Toronto Press, 1980–91), 10: 96.

17. J. S. Mill, *Utilitarianism,* 1861, ed. Roger Crisp (Oxford: Oxford University Press, 1998), 2.4.27–28, p. 56; 2.4.29, p. 56.

18. Mill, *Utilitarianism,* 2.6.18, p. 57.

19. Mill, *Utilitarianism,* 2.6.40–44, p. 57.

20. Mill, *Utilitarianism,* 2.15–16, p. 62.

21. Mill, *Utilitarianism,* 2.18.6, p. 64; 2.18.6–9, p. 64.

22. Mill, *Utilitarianism,* 17.7, p. 64.

2. Pleasure Is Good (The Epicureans)

1. Epicurus, *Letter to Menoeceus,* p. 28.

2. Lucretius, *On the Nature of the Universe,* trans. R. E. Latham (London: Penguin Books, 1951), book 3, p. 96.

3. Epicurus, *Letter to Menoeceus,* p. 29.

4. Epicurus, *Letter to Menoeceus,* p. 30.

5. Epicurus, *Letter to Menoeceus,* p. 31.

6. Cicero, *De Finibus,* trans. and ed. H. Rackham (London: William Heinemann, 1914), book 1, 41.

7. Lucretius, *On the Nature of the Universe,* book 2, p. 60.

3. Get Busy With Your Works (Hinduism)

1. *Chandogya Upanishad,* in *A Source Book in Indian Philosophy,* ed. Sarvepalli Radhakrishnan and Charles A. Moore (Princeton, NJ: Princeton University Press, 1957), pp. 69–70.

2. Ramakrishna, *Works* (Mylapore, Madras: Sri Ramakrishna Math, 1922), 1:

222–223; quoted in Troy Wilson Organ, *The Hindu Quest for the Perfection of Man* (Athens: Ohio University Press, 1970), p. 25.

3. *The Bhagavad Gita,* trans. and ed. R. C. Zaehner (London: Oxford University Press, 1966), 2.33, pp. 36–37.

4. Kim Kott, *Hinduism: A Very Short Introduction* (Oxford: Oxford University Press, 1998), p. 38.

5. Swami Vivekananda, *Bhakti-Yoga: The Yoga of Love and Devotion* (Calcutta: Advaita Ashrama, 1974), p. 31.

6. *Bhagavata Puranas,* 2.3.20–24; quoted in David N. Lorenzen, "Bhakti," in *The Hindu World,* ed. Sushil Mittal and Gene Thursby (London: Routledge, 2004), p. 194.

7. Swami Vivekananda, *Bhakti-Yoga,* p. 35.

8. *Bhakti Sutra,* 44, quoted in Organ, *The Hindu Quest for the Perfection of Man,* p. 259.

4. The Enlightened One (Buddhism)

1. *The Dhammapada,* trans. Juan Mascaró (Harmondsworth, UK: Penguin, 1973), p. 336.

2. Quoted in Vicki Mackenzie, ed., *Why Buddhism? Westerners in Search of Wisdom* (London: Thorsons, 2003), p. 265.

3. *The Dhammapada,* p. 4.

4. Mackenzie, *Why Buddhism?,* pp. 6–9.

5. Mackenzie, *Why Buddhism?,* p. 9.

6. Mackenzie, *Why Buddhism?,* pp. 259–260.

5. Only in Heaven (Christianity)

1. G. K. Chesterton, *St. Thomas Aquinas* (New York: Sheed & Ward, 1933), p. 71.

2. Thomas Aquinas, *Summa Theologiae,* part 1 of part 2, question 5, article 5, in *Treatise on Happiness,* trans. and ed. John A. Oesterle (Notre Dame, IN: University of Notre Dame Press, 1983), p. 61.

3. Aquinas, *Summa Theologiae,* part 1 of part 2, question 1, article 5, p. 10.

4. Aquinas, *Summa Theologiae,* part 1 of part 2, question 3, article 8, p. 39.

5. Aquinas, *De Potentia,* question 7, article 5, quoted in Karen Armstrong, *A History of God* (London: Vintage, 1999), p. 238.

6. Aquinas, *Summa Theologiae,* part 1 of part 2, question 3, article 2, p. 30.

7. Aquinas, *Summa Theologiae,* part 1 of part 2, question 5, article 6, p. 62.

6. The Alchemy of Happiness (Islam)

1. Abu Hamid al-Ghazali, *The Deliverance from Evil*, in W. Montgomery Watt, *The Faith and Practice of Al-Ghazali* (London: George Allen & Unwin, 1953), p. 21.
2. Ghazali, *Deliverance from Evil*, p. 55.
3. Ghazali, *Deliverance from Evil*, p. 57.
4. Ghazali, *Deliverance from Evil*, p. 76.
5. Abu Hamid al-Ghazali, *The Alchemy of Happiness*, trans. and ed. Claud Field and Elton L. Daniel (London: M.E. Sharpe, 1991), p. 52.
6. Shabistari, "The Secret Rose Garden," quoted in John Baldock, *The Essence of Sufism* (Royston, UK: Eagle Editions, 2004), p. 202.
7. Fariduddin Attar, *The Conference of the Birds*, trans. C. S. Nott (London: Routledge & Kegan Paul, 1978), p. 219.
8. Jalal al-Din Rumi, quoted in *The Wisdom of the Sufis*, ed. Kenneth Cragg (New York: New Directions, 1976), p. 13.
9. Shabistari, "The Secret Rose Garden," p. 200.

7. It's All in Your Mind (The Stoics)

1. Epictetus, *The Enchiridion*, trans. Thomas W. Higginson (New York: Macmillan, 1948), p. 9.
2. Cicero, *Tusculan Disputations*, trans. and ed. A. E. Douglas (Warminster, UK: Aris & Phillips, 1990), book 5, 12.
3. Cicero, *De Finibus*, trans. and ed. H. Rackham (London: William Heinemann, 1914), book 3, 45.
4. Cicero, *Tusculan Disputations*, book 5, 27.79.
5. Seneca, *De vita beata* 2.3, in *Seneca: Four Dialogues*, ed. C. D. N. Costa (Warminster, UK: Aris & Phillips, 1994).
6. Seneca, *De vita beata,* 10.
7. Seneca, *De vita beata,* 7.
8. Cicero, *Tusculan Disputations*, book 2, 4.1.
9. Cicero, *On Divination*, book 2, 1.1, in Cicero, *On the Good Life*, trans. and ed. Michael Grant (London: Penguin Books, 1971), p. 3.
10. Cicero, *Tusculan Disputations*, book 5, 6.16.
11. Tacitus, *Annals of Imperial Rome*, trans. and ed. Michael Grant (1956; London: Penguin Books, 1989), book 15, 62.
12. Seneca, *Consolatio ad Helviam* 5, in *Seneca: Four Dialogues*.
13. Seneca, *De vita beata,* 4.
14. *The "Meditations" of Marcus Aurelius Antoninus . . .*, ed. R. B. Rutherford, trans.

A. S. L. Farquaharson and R. B. Rutherford (Oxford: Oxford University Press, 1989), 6.30.
15. Marcus Aurelius, *Meditations,* 6.15.
16. Marcus Aurelius, *Meditations,* 8.24, 8.48.
17. Marcus Aurelius, *Meditations,* 3.6.

8. The Hidden Face of God (Judaism)

1. Eliezer Berkovits, *Faith after the Holocaust* (New York: Ktav Publishing House, 1973), p. 89.
2. Psalm 44:24–26.
3. Viktor E. Frankl, *Man's Search for Meaning* (1959; London: Random House, 2004), p. 75.
4. Frankl, *Man's Search for Meaning,* p. 75.
5. Eliezer Berkovits, *With God in Hell: Judaism in the Ghettos and Deathcamps* (New York: Sanhedrin Press, 1979), p. 111.
6. Berkovits, *With God in Hell,* p. 112.

BIBLIOGRAPHY

General Works

Argyle, Michael. *The Psychology of Happiness.* New York: Methuen, 1987.

Aristotle. *Nicomachean Ethics.* Trans. Martin Oswald. New York: Macmillan, 1962.

Barrow, Robin. *Happiness.* Oxford: Martin Robertson, 1980.

Berger, Fred R. *Happiness, Justice, and Freedom.* Berkeley: University of California Press, 1984.

Brooks, David. *Bobos in Paradise: The New Upper Class and How They Got There.* New York: Simon & Schuster, 2000.

de Bono, Edward. *The Happiness Purpose.* Harmondsworth, UK: Penguin Books, 1979.

de Botton, Alain. *The Consolations of Philosophy.* London: Hamish Hamilton, 2000.

———. *Status Anxiety.* London: Hamish Hamilton, 2004.

Dougherty, Jude P. *The Good Life and Its Pursuit.* New York: Paragon House, 1984.

Edwards, Rem B. *Pleasures and Pains: A Theory of Qualitative Hedonism.* Ithaca, NY: Cornell University Press, 1979.

Elbin, Paul Nowell. *The Paradox of Happiness.* New York: Hawthorn Books, 1975.

Eysenck, Michael W. *Happiness: Facts and Myths.* Hove, UK: Erlbaum, 1990.

Frank, Robert. *Luxury Fever: Why Money Fails to Satisfy in an Era of Excess.* New York: Free Press, 1999.

Freedman, J. *Happy People: What Happiness Is, Who Has It and Why.* New York: Harcourt, Brace, 1979.

Götz, Ignacio L. *Conceptions of Happiness.* Lanham, MD: University Press of America, 1995.

Grayling, A. C. *What Is Good? The Search for the Best Way to Live.* London: Weidenfeld & Nicholson, 2003.

Griffin, James. *Well-Being: Its Meaning, Measurement, and Moral Importance.* Oxford: Oxford University Press, 1986.

Jackson, Adam J. *The Secrets of Abundant Happiness.* London: Thorsons, 1995.

Kenny, Anthony. *Aristotle on the Perfect Life*. Oxford: Oxford University Press, 1992.

———. "Happiness." *Proceedings of the Aristotelian Society* 66 (1965–66): 93–102.

Keynes, J. M. "Economic Possibilities for Our Grandchildren." In *The Collected Writings of John Maynard Keynes*, vol. 9: 321–332. London: Macmillan, 1972.

Kingwell, Mark. *In Pursuit of Happiness: Better Living from Plato to Prozac*. New York: Crown, 1998.

Kurtz, Paul. *Exuberance: A Philosophy of Happiness*. Buffalo, NY: Prometheus Books, 1977.

Lasch, Christopher. *The Culture of Narcissism: American Life in an Age of Diminishing Expectations*. New York: Norton, 1978.

———. *The Revolt of the Elites and the Betrayal of Democracy*. New York: Norton, 1995.

Lloyd Thomas, D. A. "Happiness." *Philosophical Quarterly* 18, no. 71 (April 1968): 97–113.

Marar, Ziyad. *The Happiness Paradox*. London: Reaktion Books, 2003.

McFall, Lynne. *Happiness*. New York: Peter Lang, 1979.

McGill, Vivian. *The Idea of Happiness*. New York: Frederick A. Praeger, 1967.

McMahon, Darrin. *Happiness: A History*. New York: Grove Atlantic, 2006.

Montague, Roger. "Happiness." *Proceedings of the Aristotelian Society* 67 (1966–67): 87–102.

Morris, Desmond. *Happiness*. Birmingham, UK: University of Birmingham Press, 1984.

Murray, Charles. *In Pursuit of Happiness and Good Government*. New York: Simon & Schuster, 1988.

Nozick, Robert. *The Examined Life: Philosophical Meditations*. New York: Simon & Schuster, 1989.

Nussbaum, Martha, and Amartya Sen, eds. *The Quality of Life*. Oxford: Oxford University Press, 1992.

Pieper, Josef. *Happiness and Contemplation*. New York: Pantheon, 1958.

———. *In Defense of Philosophy*. San Francisco: Ignatius Press, 1992.

Powys, John Cowper. *The Art of Happiness*. New York: Simon & Schuster, 1935.

Putnam, Robert D. *Bowling Alone: The Collapse and Revival of American Community*. New York: Touchstone, 2000.

Rouner, Leroy S., ed. *In Pursuit of Happiness*. South Bend, IN: Notre Dame University Press, 1995.

Russell, Bertrand. *The Conquest of Happiness*. London: George Allen & Unwin, 1958.

Sachs, Hanns. "Psychotherapy and the Pursuit of Happiness." *Imago* 1 (1939): 356–364.

Samuelson, Robert J. *The Good Life and Its Discontents: The American Dream in the Age of Entitlement.* New York: Vintage, 1995.

Simpson, Robert W. "Happiness." *American Philosophical Quarterly* (April 1975): 169–176.

Sumner, L. Wayne. "Welfare, Happiness and Pleasure." *Utilitas* 4, no. 2 (November 1992): 199–223.

Telfer, Elizabeth. *Happiness.* New York: St. Martin's Press, 1980.

Tolstoy, Leo. *A Confession and Other Religious Writings.* Trans. Jane Kentish. London: Penguin Books, 1987.

White, Stephen A. *Sovereign Virtue: Aristotle on the Relation between Happiness and Prosperity.* Stanford: Stanford University Press, 1992.

Wike, Victoria S. *Kant on Happiness in Ethics.* Albany: State University of New York Press, 1994.

The "New Science" of Happiness

Biswas-Diener, Robert, Ed Diener, and Maya Tamir, "The Psychology of Subjective Well-being." *Daedalus* (spring 2004): 18–25.

Csikszentmihalyi, Mihalyi. *Flow: The Psychology of Optimal Experience.* New York: Harper & Row, 1990.

———. *Living Well: The Psychology of Everyday Life.* New York: Basic Books, 1997.

Diener, Ed, and E. Suh, eds. *Culture and Subjective Well-being.* Cambridge, MA: MIT Press, 2000.

Easterlin, Richard A. "The Economics of Happiness." *Daedalus* (spring 2004): 26–33.

———, ed. *Happiness in Economics.* Cheltenham, UK: Edward Elgar, 2002.

Frey, Bruno S., and Alois Stutzer. *Happiness and Economics: How the Economy and Institutions Affect Well-being.* Princeton, NJ: Princeton University Press, 2002.

Kahneman, Daniel, Ed Diener, and Norbert Schwarz, eds. *Well-being: The Foundations of Hedonic Psychology.* New York: Russell Sage Foundation, 1999.

Layard, Richard. *Happiness: Lessons from a New Science.* London: Allen Lane, 2005.

Martin, Paul. *Making Happy People.* London: Fourth Estate, 2005.

Nettle, Daniel. *Happiness: The Science behind Your Smile.* Oxford: Oxford University Press, 2005.

"Richer Not Happier: A 21st-Century Search for the Good Life." *Royal Society for the Arts Journal* (July 2004): 36–45.

Seligman, Martin. *Authentic Happiness.* New York: Free Press, 2002.

Tomkins, Richard. "How to Be Happy." *Financial Times,* 8–9 March 2003.

Veenhoven, Ruut. *Conditions of Happiness.* Dordecht, Netherlands: D. Reidel, 1984.

Epicureanism

Annas, Julia. *The Morality of Happiness.* New York: Oxford University Press, 1993.
Cicero, Marcus Tullius. *On the Ends of Goods and Evils (De Finibus . . .).* Trans. and ed. H. Rackham. London: William Heinemann, 1914.
———. *Tusculan Disputations.* Trans. and ed. A. E. Douglas. Warminster, UK: Aris & Phillips, 1990.
DeWitt, Norman Wentworth. *Epicurus and His Philosophy.* Minneapolis: University of Minnesota Press, 1954.
Diogenes Laertius. *Lives of the Philosophers.* Trans. R. D. Hicks. Cambridge, MA: Harvard University Press, 1958.
Epicurus. *Letters, Principal Doctrines,* and *Vatican Sayings.* In *The Epicurus Reader: Selected Writings and Testiminia.* Trans. and ed. Brad Inwood and L. P. Gerson. Cambridge, MA: Hackett, 1994.
Hibler, Richard. *Happiness through Tranquillity: The School of Epicurus.* Lanham, MD: University Press of America, 1984.
Lucretius. *On the Nature of the Universe.* Trans. R. E. Latham. London: Penguin Books, 1951.
Rist, J. M. *Epicurus: An Introduction.* Cambridge, UK: Cambridge University Press, 1972.
Strodach, George K., ed. *The Philosophy of Epicurus.* Evanston, IL: Northwestern University Press, 1963.

Utilitarianism

Barrow, Robin. *Utilitariansim.* Brookfield, VT: Edward Elgar, 1991.
Bentham, Jeremy. *An Introduction to the Principles of Morals and Legislation.* 1791. Ed. J. H. Burns and H. L. A. Hart. Oxford: Oxford University Press, 1996.
Capaldi, Nicholas. *John Stuart Mill: A Biography.* Cambridge, UK: Cambridge University Press, 2004.
Ebenstein, Alan O. *The Greatest Happiness Principle: An Examination of Utilitarianism.* New York: Garland, 1991.
Hobbes, Thomas. *Leviathan.* Ed. Michael Oakeshott. New York: Macmillan, 1962.
Mill, J. S. *Autobiography of John Stuart Mill.* New York: Columbia University Press, 1924.
———. *Utilitarianism.* 1861. Ed. Roger Crisp. Oxford: Oxford University Press, 1998.
Quinton, Anthony. *Utilitarian Ethics,* 2nd ed. London: Duckworth, 1989.
Robson, J. M., ed., et al. *The Philosophy of John Stuart Mill.* Toronto: University of Toronto Press, 1980.

Ryan, Alan. *J. S. Mill.* London: Routledge & Kegan Paul, 1974.
———. *The Philosophy of John Stuart Mill.* London: Macmillan, 1970.

Hinduism

The Bhagavad-Gita. Trans. and ed. R. C. Zaehner. London: Oxford University Press, 1966.

Chaudhuri, Haridas. *Integral Yoga: The Concept of Harmonious and Creative Living.* London: George Allen & Unwin, 1965.

Flood, Gavin. *An Introduction to Hinduism.* Cambridge, UK: Cambridge University Press, 1996.

Hamilton, Sue. *Indian Philosophy: A Very Short Introduction.* Oxford: Oxford University Press, 2001.

Klostermaier, Klaus K. *A Survey of Hinduism.* Albany: State University of New York Press, 1994.

Kott, Kim. *Hinduism: A Very Short Introduction.* Oxford: Oxford University Press, 1998.

Mittal, Sushil, and Gene Thursby, eds. *The Hindu World.* London: Routledge, 2004.

Organ, Troy Wilson. *The Hindu Quest for the Perfection of Man.* Athens: Ohio University Press, 1970.

Pandit, M. P. *The Yoga of Knowledge.* Pomona, CA: Auromere, 1979.

Panigrahi, Sarat Chandra. *The Concept of Yoga in "The Gita."* Puri, Orissa, India: Prajnaloka, 1994.

Prem, Sri Krishna. *The Yoga of "The Bhagavat Gita."* London: John M. Watkins, 1951.

Radhakrishnan, Sarvepalli, and Charles A. Moore, eds. *A Sourcebook in Indian Philosophy.* Princeton, NJ: Princeton University Press, 1957.

Satchidananda, Swami, ed. *Living Yoga: The Value of Yoga in Today's Life.* New York: Gordon and Breach Science Publishers, 1976.

Vivekananda, Swami. *Bhakti-Yoga: The Yoga of Love and Devotion.* Calcutta: Advaita Ashrama, 1974.

Zaehner, R. C. *Hindu and Muslim Mysticism.* Oxford: Oneworld Publications, 1960.

Buddhism

Armstrong, Karen. *Buddha.* 2000. London: Orion Books, 2002.

Carrithers, Michael. *Buddha: A Very Short Introduction.* 1983. Oxford: Oxford University Press, 2001.

Coleman, James William. *The New Buddhism: The Western Transformation of an Ancient Tradition.* Oxford: Oxford University Press, 2001.

Conradi, Peter J. *Going Buddhist*. London: Short Books, 2004.

Cope, Stephen. *Yoga and the Quest for the True Self*. New York: Bantam Books, 1999.

Dalai Lama, His Holiness. *Ancient Wisdom, Modern World: Ethics for a New Millennium*. London: Little, Brown, 1999.

Dalai Lama, His Holiness, and Howard C. Cutler. *The Art of Happiness: A Handbook for Living*. London: Hodder and Stoughton, 1998.

The Dhammapada. Trans. Juan Mascaró. Harmondsworth, UK: Penguin, 1973.

Dumoulion, Heinrich, and John C. Maraldo, eds. *Buddhism in the Modern World*. New York: Macmillan, 1976.

Humphreys, Christmas. *Exploring Buddhism*. London: George Allen & Unwin, 1974.

Keown, Damien. *Buddhism: A Very Short Introduction*. Oxford: Oxford University Press, 1996.

LaFleur, William R. *Buddhism*. Englewood Cliffs, NJ: Prentice-Hall, 1988.

Lopez, Donald S., Jr. *Buddhism*. London: Penguin Press, 2001.

Mackenzie, Vicki, ed. *Why Buddhism? Westerners in Search of Wisdom*. London: Thorsons, 2003.

Mitchell, Donald W. *Buddhism: Introducing the Buddhist Experience*. New York: Oxford University Press, 2002.

Christianity

Armstrong, Karen. *A History of God*. 1993. London: Vintage, 1999.

Chesterton, G. K. *St. Thomas Aquinas*. New York: Sheed & Ward, 1933.

Cupitt, Don. *Mysticism after Modernity*. Oxford: Blackwell, 1998.

Pieper, Josef. *The Silence of St. Thomas*. South Bend, IN: St. Augustine's Press, 1999.

Thomas Aquinas. *St. Thomas Aquinas on Politics and Ethics*. Trans. and ed. Paul E. Sigmund. New York: Norton, 1988.

———. *Treatise on Happiness*. Trans. and ed. John A. Oesterle. Notre Dame, IN: University of Notre Dame Press, 1983.

———. *Virtue: Way to Happiness*. Trans. Richard J. Regan. Scranton, PA: University of Scranton Press, 1999.

Weisheipl, J. *Friar Thomas D'Aquino: His Life, Thought, and Works*. Washington, DC: Catholic University of America Press, 1983.

Islam

al-Ghazali, Abu Hamid. *The Alchemy of Happiness*. Trans. and ed. Claud Field and Elton L. Daniel. London: M.E. Sharpe, 1991.

Armstrong, Karen. *A History of God*. 1993. London: Vintage, 1999.

Attar, Fariduddin. *The Conference of the Birds.* Trans. C. S. Nott. London: Routledge & Kegan Paul, 1978.

Baldock, John. *The Essence of Sufism.* Royston, UK: Eagle Editions, 2004.

Cragg, Kenneth, ed. *The Wisdom of the Sufis.* New York: New Directions, 1976.

Fakhry, Majid. *A History of Islamic Philosophy.* London: Longman, 1983.

Macdonald, Duncan B. "The Life of al-Ghazali." *Journal of the American Oriental Society* 20 (1899): 71–132.

Nasr, Seyyed Hossein. *Living Sufism.* London: Mandala Books, 1980.

Quasem, Muhammad Abul. "Al-Ghazali's Conception of Happiness." *Arabica* 22 (1975): 153–161.

———. *The Ethics of Al-Ghazali: A Composite Ethics in Islam.* Selangor, Malaysia: Peninsular Malaysia, 1975.

Shabistari. "The Secret Rose Garden." Trans. Florence Lederer. Grand Rapids, MI: Phanes Press, 1987.

Shah, Idries. *The Sufis.* London: Octagon Press, 1964.

Sharif, M. M., ed. *A History of Muslim Philosophy.* 2 vols. Delhi: Low Price Publications, 1961.

Sheikh, M. Saeed. *Studies in Muslim Philosophy.* Lahore, Pakistan: Ashraf Press, 1962.

Sherif, Mohamed Ahmed. *Ghazali's Theory of Virtue.* Albany: State University of New York Press, 1975.

Smith, Margaret. *Al-Ghazali the Mystic.* London: Luzac, 1944.

Umaruddin, M. *The Ethical Philosophy of Al-Ghazzali.* Aligarh, India: Aligarh Muslim University Press, 1962.

Watt, W. Montgomery. *The Faith and Practice of Al-Ghazali.* London: George Allen & Unwin, 1953. (The text includes a translation of Ghazali's *The Deliverance from Evil.*)

———. *Muslim Intellectual: A Study of Al-Ghazali.* Edinburgh, Scotland: Edinburgh University Press, 1963.

Zaehner, R. C. *Hindu and Muslim Mysticism.* Oxford: Oneworld Publications, 1960.

Stoicism

Boethius. *The Consolation of Philosophy.* Trans. Richard Green. New York: Macmillan, 1962.

Cicero, Marcus Tullius. *On the Ends of Goods and Evils* (*De Finibus . . .*). Trans. and ed. H. Rackham. London: William Heinemann, 1914.

———. *On the Good Life.* Trans. and ed. Michael Grant. London: Penguin Books, 1971.

————. *Stoic Paradoxes*. Trans. and ed. M. R. Wright. Warminster, UK: Aris & Phillips, 1991.

————. *Tusculan Disputations*. Trans. and ed. A. E. Douglas. Warminster, UK: Aris & Phillips, 1990.

Colish, Marcia L. *The Stoic Tradition from Antiquity to the Early Middle Ages*. Leiden, Netherlands: E.J. Brill, 1985.

Edelstein, Ludwig. *The Meaning of Stoicism*. Cambridge, MA: Harvard University Press, 1966.

Epictetus. *The Enchiridion*. Trans. Thomas W. Higginson. New York: Macmillan, 1948.

Long, A. A. *Stoic Studies*. Cambridge, UK: Cambridge University Press, 1996.

————, ed. *Hellenistic Philosophy*. Berkeley: University of California Press, 1986.

Marcus Aurelius. *The "Meditations" of Marcus Aurelius Antoninus* . . . Ed. R. B. Rutherford. Trans. A. S. L. Farquaharson and R. B. Rutherford. Oxford: Oxford University Press, 1989.

Seneca. *Consolatio ad Helviam* and *De vita beata*. In *Seneca: Four Dialogues*. Ed. C. D. N. Costa. Warminster, UK: Aris & Phillips, 1994.

Sorabji, Richard. *Emotion and Peace of Mind: From Stoic Agitation to Christian Temptation*. Oxford: Oxford University Press, 2000.

Sørensen, Villy. *Seneca: The Humanist at the Court of Nero*. Edinburgh, Scotland: Canongate, 1984.

Stockdale, James B. "Testing Epictetus' Doctrine in a Laboratory of Human Behaviour." *Bulletin of the Institute of Classical Studies* 40 (1995): 1–13.

————. *A Vietnam Experience: Ten Years of Reflection*. Stanford: Hoover Institution, 1984.

Strange, Steven K., and Jack Zupko, eds. *Stoicism: Traditions and Transformations*. Cambridge, UK: Cambridge University Press, 2004.

Tacitus. *The Annals of Imperial Rome*. Trans. and ed. Michael Grant. 1956. London: Penguin Books, 1989.

Wenley, R. M. *Stoicism and Its Influence*. New York: Cooper Square Publishers, 1963.

Judaism

Andersen, Francis I. *Job: An Introduction and Commentary*. Leicester, UK: Inter-Varsity Press, 1976.

Berkovits, Eliezer. *Faith after the Holocaust*. New York: Ktav Publishing House, 1973.

————. *God, Man and History: A Jewish Interpretation*. New York: Jonathan David, 1959.

————. *With God in Hell*. New York: Sanhedrin Press, 1979.

Frank, Daniel H., and Oliver Leaman, eds. *History of Jewish Philosophy.* London: Routledge, 1997.

Frankl, Viktor E. *Man's Search for Meaning.* 1959. London: Random House, 2004.

Habel, Norman C. *The Book of Job: A Commentary.* London: SCM Press, 1985.

Kushner, Harold S. *When Bad Things Happen to Good People.* 1981. London: Pan Macmillan, 2002.

Perdue, L. G., and W. C. Gilpin, eds. *The Voice from the Whirlwind: Interpreting the Book of Job.* Nashville, TN: Abingdon Press, 1992.

Samuelson, Norbert M. *An Introduction to Modern Jewish Philosophy.* Albany: State University of New York Press, 1989.

INDEX

ABOUT THE AUTHOR

Richard Schoch is Professor of the History of Culture at Queen Mary, University of London, where he is also Director of the Graduate School in Humanities and Social Sciences. His most recent book is *Queen Victoria and the Theatre of Her Age.* His earlier books, *Not Shakespeare* and *Shakespeare's Victorian Stage,* were shortlisted, respectively, for the Theatre Book Prize (UK) and the Barnard Hewitt Award (US). He is the recipient of fellowships from the Whiting Foundation, the Folger Shakespeare Library, the Stanford Humanities Center, and the Leverhulme Trust and is a regular reviewer for the *Times Literary Supplement* and commentator for the BBC. Prior to his academic career, he studied world history and culture with the Jesuits, wrote copy for NBC's flagship television station in New York's Rockefeller Center, and managed development projects in Morocco and Tunisia. He is happy to have received an indulgence for his sins from Pope John Paul I.

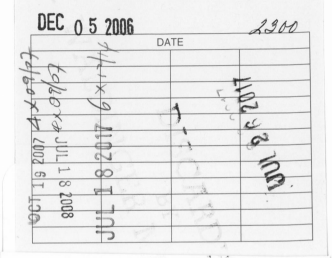